Classic CAJUN DEUX

More Culture & Cooking

By: Lucy Henry Zaunbrecher

The Front Cover Photograph is by Hillary McKoin-Bayer, Wilmot, Arkansas. A graduate of Louisiana Tech with degrees in Graphic Design and Photography, she is currently self-employed in graphic design and photography.

ISBN: 0-9640748-1-8

Copyright©2002 Lucy Henry Zaunbrecher

1st Printing   February 2003
2nd Printing   December 2004

WIMMER
COOKBOOKS

A CONSOLIDATED GRAPHICS COMPANY

800.548.2537   wimmerco.com

Merci Beaucoup

Merci beaucoup to all my family and friends who have helped me to become who I am today (a good cook). You are the main ingredients in my recipe for life.

Ms. Lucy

Grand mere

Frozine Foreman Richard
1880-1950

Mama

Eloise R. Henry

Eloise Richard Henry
1910-1991

Lucy Henry Zaunbrecher

Lucy Henry Zaunbrecher
1938-

Lucy McKenzie

Lucy Suzanne Mckenzie
1991-

247 years ago, an event took place that molded the future of Louisiana. That was when my ancestors ventured into this beautiful and very fruitful state. The Henris and Richards were part of the "great derangement." Little did they know what influence that would have on me as a Cajun. I am very proud of my heritage which was handed down to me. Now, I am proud to hand it down from my grandparents and parents to my children and my precious granddaughter. Where I live and who I am is part of Ms. Lucy's Classic Cajun Culture and Cooking.

Introduction to how this book came to life

The Executive Producer of Louisiana Public Broadcasting told me I should write another cookbook. So I started to try to gather my recipes to send to my printing company. As I was doing so, I also went about my housekeeping chores. Well, one day, I ventured into one of my closets to clean it out. I came across this old rusty looking filing cabinet. As I opened it, I could not believe what I found! It was an old filing box that contained a bunch of some recipes I had in high school plus a treasure of my mother's recipes in her own handwriting. These are all priceless and were the answer to my prayer to make this book as good as my first one.

As I read through every one very carefully, I relived the days of yesteryear. My heart is heavy yet it rejoices as I make this collection of recipes a part of my new series, Ms. Lucy's Classic Cajun Culture and Cooking show and my precious *Classic Cajun Culture and Cooking Deux*.

Enjoy! and Bon Appetit!

Ms. Lucy

Getting to Know Ms. Lucy

Born in the southwest Louisiana town of Gueydan, Lucy grew up on her parent's rice farm. At a young age, her mother, Mary Eloise Richard Henry, taught Lucy how to use the rice, poultry, beef, pork, vegetables and seafood indigenous to Louisiana to create simple, yet delicious Cajun meals.

The joy of preparing a meal for family and friends has always been a tradition in her family, one she continued after marrying her childhood sweetheart Harry John Zaunbrecher.

In an effort to preserve her family's great recipes, Lucy compiled a cookbook called *Classic Cajun Culture and Cooking* in 1994. Her inspiration was to pass on her Cajun culture and cooking to her granddaughter Lucy. It must have worked because eight-year-old Lucy now joins Grandma in the kitchen for some of the cooking segments in her show.

"Although it took only six months of work, I felt like I had given birth!" Lucy said. "What a great experience and feeling of accomplishment!"

Her friends encouraged Lucy to start selling her cookbook on local television and the result was her half-hour cooking show, **Ms. Lucy's Classic Cajun Culture and Cooking.** After two years on commercial TV, Lucy joined the Louisiana Public Broadcasting family of great cooks. After shortening the title to **Lucy's Classic Cajun Culture and Cooking,** the program was syndicated through the National Educational Telecommunications Association (NETA) to public television stations around the country.

This little country girl's cooking expertise and infectious personality have taken her to places she never could have imagined when she was a child growing up in Louisiana. She has taught cooking students in Norway and Sweden to prepare Shrimp Étouffée and other Cajun delicacies and lectured in Fond du Lac, Wisconsin, on making the perfect Roux. While she was in Wisconsin, she also gave a lecture to the French Club at a local high school that went so well it was expanded from one hour to two.

"I have traveled extensively during the last few years promoting Cajun culture and cooking, which is my precious heritage," Lucy said. "I have received many awards, but the best award is finding and making so many new friends."

Cooking the Cajun Way

Cajuns specialize in plain, simple meals which are filling and tasty for country folk. They take cooking and foods seriously and take great pride in them.

Cajuns don't make a lot of different salads because they seldom eat them. In the few salads they do make, they never peel the tomatoes or remove their seeds. Also, they always season their meats before putting them in the pot to cook.

Appetizers are also rare in Cajun kitchens. Very seldom, if ever, is an appetizer served since the Cajuns fear it would only ruin their appetite before a good meal.

Cajuns love sweets but rarely eat dessert after a hearty meal.

Cajun cooking may be time consuming, but it is well worth what you put into it. It has to be. Cajuns love eating their foods as much as they love preparing them.

To truly understand Cajun food, you have to understand the Cajun people. That's why I've incorporated photos and stories of the people throughout this book.

I've also provided the following essay on the Cajun people in an effort to further understanding of their unique culture.

Cajuns — Who They Are

To the uninitiated, a Cajun is a crude ignorant backwoodsman who speaks little or no English. He makes his living fishing, trapping or farming a few acres of land and his principal interests are boozing, eating and having a good time.

Perhaps there are such people in Acadiana, but they are an infinitesimal minority and are in no way characteristic of the Cajun people.

Instead, Cajuns have a long and proud heritage on this continent. This heritage began in 1604 when the first French settler colonized Nova Scotia. Much like America's first colonists, they fought to civilize a new world, bringing the culture and language of France to their adopted land.

England gained control of Nova Scotia with the Treaty of Utrech in 1713 and life became unbearable for the Cajuns. As French Catholics living under the rule of English Protestants, the Cajuns found themselves despised and persecuted. Between 6,000 and 7,000 were deported to the American colonies. However, most of these

colonies also had laws prohibiting Catholics to live within their borders, so life didn't get much better.

Others sought refuge in the Caribbean or among the Indians of the American wilderness. Others, deported to England, eventually found their way to France.

Refugees from all these groups eventually found their way to Louisiana. There, they founded their own communities. In a climate unlike any they'd known before, surrounded by plants and animals for which they had no names in their language, the Cajuns created a new language and a new culture. It even became necessary to create a new way of cooking since many of the ingredients they'd known were unavailable — replaced by the abundant seafood and game of south Louisiana. Small, family-owned stores and meat markets still exist in southwest Louisiana in testimony to the impact this had on the lives of the Cajuns.

When the Acadiens came into the bayou country from New Orleans, the Indians here could not pronounce "Acadien." Therefore, the name "Cajun" was adopted because it was easier to pronounce.

However, the words Cajun and Acadien do not have the same meaning. The word Cajun applies only to those whose Acadien ancestors came to Louisiana after the eviction of 1755. The broader term, Acadien, applies to all the descendants of the original Acadiens, regardless of where they live. Thus, all Cajuns are Acadiens, but not all Acadiens are Cajuns.

Many thousands of Acadiens live in different parts of the United States and Canada. These are not Cajuns. By extension, the title of Cajun is properly applied to those people (regardless of national origin) who have intermarried with Cajuns and have been absorbed into the Cajun culture and speak the Cajun language. This is why my husband is classified as a Cajun even though his name is Zaunbrecher and he is of German descent.

Today, historians agree that the culture the Cajuns developed is one of the most unique and impressive in the world. They also agree that the Cajuns have played a significant role in American history as they struggled to survive.

Throughout this rebirth of Acadiana, the Cajuns stuck together. They minded their own business, kept apart from the rest of the world and supported each other.

In the 20th century, oil brought riches to the Cajuns. Yet even this couldn't change them much.

Today, they are as they always were: fun-loving, God-fearing, hard-working. Over a million of these French-speaking people exist in our country today, a tribute to their determination and the power of the human will.

In spite of the tribulations they've endured, today's Cajuns still maintain a joie-de-vivre and a live-and-let-live attitude which is admired by all who know them. They are ready with a smile, a joke and a handshake for anyone willing to accept it. They'll give you the shirt off their back or the beer out of their glass.

That is who a Cajun is.

Cajuns and Not Creoles

I've often been asked to explain the difference between Cajuns and Creoles.

This basically comes down to a question of style. Creole cooking is a more sophisticated, city cousin of Cajun cooking. Both come from the same roots.

Both Cajun and Creole cuisines were found and brought together by their French roots, livened with spices from Spain, inspired by African vegetables, Caribbeanized by West Indian hands, laced with black pepper and pork by the Germans, infiltrated with potatoes by the Irish, blasted with tomatoes and garlic by the Italians and also touched in a small way by the Swiss, Dutch, Malayans and Malaysians.

What a complex taste!

The Creoles have sauces and delicious soups beyond describing. Their brunches are luscious. The "Haute" (up town) manner of wining and dining reflects the dignified French social groups of Creoles.

Many different courses are also served.

The French from France married with the Spanish and their direct descendants were Creoles. However, many ethnic groups were brought in, diluting the Creole race. New Orleans is the "Heart" of Creole country, the same as Breaux Bridge and Lafayette are the "Heart" of Cajun Country.

This classic lady, my mama, gave me the inspiration it took for me to materialize my talent for cooking. Had it not been for her, I would have missed a beautiful part in my life. The only physical image I have of her is this photo which Melissa, my daughter, took of her at the beautiful age of 80 years young. But she will remain in my heart forever.

Table of Contents

First You Make A Roux

First you make a roux! Sound familiar?

What is a roux? Well, to me, it is the foundation of many Cajun dishes.

A roux is a mixture of flour and oil slowly cooked to a perfect uniform brown color. Most of the rouxs consist of equal parts of flour and oil (one cup oil plus one cup flour).

I always allow the oil to get hot before adding the flour — this speeds up the cooking time of the roux. A medium high heat is recommended. The slower the roux is cooked, the better the flavor. Beginners should use a medium heat and only experts should cook a roux on high heat.

As soon as the required color is formed, turn off the heat and add the sliced or chopped onions to the roux. Since the onions cannot burn, it will cool off the roux so that the desired color is retained and the roux will not burn nor get darker. However, you must continue to stir the roux even though the heat is off.

Some dishes do not require onions. In that case, remove the roux from the heat and continue to stir until it has cooled. You may also place the pot in cold water to help cool it down.

Learning the process of making a roux is half the challenge of becoming a good Cajun cook.

Basic Roux

1 cup oil

1 cup flour

**Water for gumbo or gravy (2-3 quarts for gumbo;
1 quart for gravy)**

Pour oil into a thick, heavy pot, stirring constantly; add flour, being careful not to burn. If you notice some black specks in your roux, just throw it away and start anew. The specks give it a bitter taste which, as far as I know, cannot be remedied.

A whisk is a wonderful tool to use in preparing a roux but be careful of the edges around the pot — use a spoon to stir on the sides occasionally to scrape loose the flour.

Cook on medium high heat until the desired color has been obtained. A dark roux of dark chocolate color is required to use for gumbos, stews and sauce piquantes. A lighter roux which resembles the color of peanut butter is required for étouffées or light gravies.

Once the right color is obtained, add the required amount of water, stirring constantly. Bring to a fast boil, then lower the heat to a slow boil until the right thickness is obtained.

A roux can be made and stored in a refrigerator for months. If you keep it to be used later, do not add any water but continue to stir after the heat has been turned off until it cools down.

It will be very thick and pasty. Store in a covered container. When needed, remove the amount you need and stir into a quart of boiling water until it is all dissolved.

Roux is definitely not to be eaten alone, but is absolutely necessary for most Cajun specialties. Roux is a big asset to a dish as it is used as a thickener and a flavoring agent.

In a Cajun kitchen, herbs, seasonings and spices are used to enhance the taste of the main ingredient (fish, pork, beef, poultry, etc.) A Cajun always pours off excess fat in a dish to "de-glace" the pan. (Pour in a little water and scrape loose the browned part to add flavor and make a gravy.)

Since I was born and raised on a rice farm and then later became a rice producer myself, it is no surprise that you find this recipe in my section. Rice was served every day at my home and is still served that often. It is prepared along with potatoes and beans or simply covered with good gravy. Rice is economical to prepare and is very versatile. A meal at home isn't complete without it.

I sometimes use a rice cooker, making it easy to cook. Most of the time, however, I prepare it the old way. Regardless, I add 1 teaspoon of vinegar per 3 cups of rice (adding it to the water after it's been measured). This helps the kernels to hold firm and gives them a beautiful white, clean look. The butter or margarine gives it a fuller, richer flavor and keeps it from sticking to the bottom of the pot. Both are really optional.

Another method of cooking rice — one not widely known or seen in cookbooks—is to use a spaghetti cooker or steamer. I started using this method when my husband was diagnosed for diabetes. Removing starch from the diet is best for diabetics since it converts immediately to sugar when in the bloodstream.

Rinse 3 cups of rice in a spaghetti cooker or steamer insert. Replace the insert onto the pot. Add 6 to 8 cups of water and 1 teaspoon of vinegar. Bring to a boil and continue boiling until the kernels double in size (this takes about 15 minutes) and appear done. I usually taste to see if it's done. Then pull the insert out of the pot, drain the starchy water and rinse off the excess starches by putting the insert under a cold water faucet and allowing the water to run through the rice while you stir it. Then replace the insert inside the pot and allow to drain. When ready to serve, reheat the amount needed in a microwave or warm slowly over a low flame. The grains will just roll apart and they taste so good.

Refrigerate all the leftover rice. It will keep for as long as a week if tightly covered, and can be frozen indefinitely.

Other Ways To Prepare Rice

1   **cup regular milled long grain rice**
2   **cups water or other liquid**
1   **tablespoon butter**
      Takes 15 minutes.
      <u>**OR**</u>

1   **cup regular milled medium or short grain rice**
1¾   **cups water or other liquid**
1   **tablespoon butter**
      Takes 15 minutes.
      <u>**OR**</u>

1   **cup brown rice**
2½   **cups water or other liquid**
1   **tablespoon butter**
      Takes 45-50 minutes.
      <u>**OR**</u>

1   **cup parboiled rice**
2½   **cups water or other liquid**
1   **tablespoon butter**
      Takes 20-25 minutes.

Combine rice, liquid and butter in 2-3 quart saucepan. Bring to a hard boil. Stir once or twice. Reduce heat, cover and simmer for specified time. If rice is not tender or liquid is not all absorbed, replace lid and cook 2-4 minutes longer. Fluff with fork. Serves 2-3.

Liquids other than water can be used to attain different flavors. Suggestions are chicken or beef stocks, bullion, consomme, tomato or other vegetable juices, or fruit juice. If juices are used, add one part water to 1 part juice. Recommended juices are apple and orange.

To microwave rice, combine rice, liquid and butter in a 2-3 quart deep microwave baking dish. Cover with an absorbent towel, and cook on high for 5 minutes or until boiling. Reduce heat to medium and cook 15 minutes longer for parboiled rice or 30 minutes longer for brown rice. Fluff with a fork.

Gumbo is the Cajun's favorite dish for family and friends. It is very typical of a Cajun to say, "Ya'll come over and we'll make a big pot of gumbo." Gumbo is a one-dish, main course meal.

Every year, we attended Christmas midnight mass. Then, after the services, we always went home to a pot of chicken gumbo which my mother had prepared before we went to church.

So, as the song says, "Jambalaya, crawfish pie, filé gumbo!" Gumbo always reflects a celebration or a good time with friends or relatives or both. That is why the gumbo pot is a big one and every kitchen is equipped with one of those.

The following recipe comes from an interview in "Les Acadien D'Asteur" by Philip Gould.

You start with some oil in your pot. And then you make your roux with some flour, white flour, you know. Then, you peel your onion. You cut it fine, fine. Then when your roux is browned, then you take your onion and you brown it with your roux. Then, if you want to make a gallon of gumbo, you put about a gallon water in it to boil.

Then, you brown your chicken on the side. And then you put your chicken in it, into your gumbo. And you let it simmer for about an hour and a half, or an hour. On a low fire, you want to put it. If it's an old hen, it takes maybe like two hours to make your gumbo. And if it's a young chicken, it doesn't take as long. And then, instead of putting in chicken, you can just put seafood if you want. It's just as good and maybe better. But that, you have to put in at the very end, just before it's finished.

Then you put in your salt, your black pepper and your cayenne. You season it like you like it. You can put red peppers or green peppers, or both. Like you want. That's up to you. Then, you taste it to see if it's seasoned enough. That's when you're ready, about 15, 20 minutes before putting out your fire, you chop your parsley and your onion tops. And you put them in there, in your gumbo, just about 15 minutes before your gumbo is cooked. And then, that's all. Your gumbo is ready! Then it's all right. When you're ready to serve it in your bowls, you put your filé. Then you eat it with rice in your bowls.

GUMBO

Soups/ Gumbo

Soups and gumbos are so easy to make and are so delicious for any occasion! I always make a big pot of soup or gumbo because it seems like the bigger the pot, the better it tastes! Whether it's for the whole family or only for a sick member, I always enjoy preparing and serving this – besides, it is an easy clean-up with only one pot to wash!

Salmon Gumbo

½	cup flour
½	cup canola oil
1	onion, chopped
1	bell pepper, chopped
½	cup chopped celery
2	14½ ounce cans fat-free chicken broth
1	cup water
2	15 ounce cans salmon
¾	cup chopped green onions
	Tony Chachere's More Spice seasoning to taste

Mix flour into oil in a pot and cook to make a dark roux. Add onions, bell pepper and celery. Cook 2 to 3 minutes. Add broth and water. Cook over medium heat about 20 minutes. Add salmon and simmer 30 minutes, adding green onions during the last 10 minutes. Serve with freshly cooked rice.

Corn Soup

2½	cups fresh corn
1	pound smoked sausage (homemade is best), sliced
1	onion, chopped
1	bell pepper, chopped
2	stalks celery, chopped
3	tablespoons bacon fat
2	14½ ounce cans chicken broth
½	10 ounce can Rotel tomatoes
2	8 ounce cans tomato sauce

Smother corn, sausage, onions, bell pepper and celery in bacon fat for about 20 minutes. Add broth, tomatoes and tomato sauce. Simmer 1 to 1½ hours. Serve with cornbread.

Shrimp-Okra Gumbo

4   pounds fresh okra, cut into ¼-inch pieces,
    or 5 (16 ounce) cans
2   large tomatoes, peeled and chopped
2   medium onions, chopped
¼   cup oil
2   quarts water
    salt and pepper to taste
3   pounds shrimp, peeled and deveined

Cook okra, tomatoes and onions in oil for 45 to 60 minutes or until okra is not stringy or slimy. Add water and season with salt and pepper. Simmer 30 minutes. Add shrimp and cook 10 to 15 minutes longer. Serve over cooked rice. Serves 6.

This was another favorite of mine. Mrs. Ollie Linscombe cooked this to perfection. She was a very dear friend and the mother of one of my sister's-in-law. She will long be remembered as a great cook and a very sweet lady.

Crawfish Corn Soup

1½ cups chopped green onion tops
1   cup chopped fresh mushrooms
4   tablespoons margarine
1   8 ounce package cream cheese
2   10½ ounce cans condensed cream of potato
    soup
1   10¾ ounce can condensed cream of
    mushroom soup
2   16 ounce cans whole kernel corn (1 can white
    corn, 1 can yellow)
1   pound crawfish tailmeat
1   pint half-and-half
    salt and pepper to taste
    Louisiana red pepper sauce to taste

Mary Stevens cooks this dish for friends and relatives. I am so happy I am her friend and that she shared this recipe with me (as well as the soup).

Sauté green onions and mushrooms in margarine. Soften cream cheese in microwave and add to sautéed vegetables. Cook over medium-low heat. Add soups and corn. Mix well. Stir in crawfish. Add half-and-half and season with salt, pepper and pepper sauce. Cook 25 to 30 minutes. Serves 4 to 6.

y friend, Chef Hans,
ught me how to cook
is when I helped him at
wedding reception. I
ve it and eat it as often
s I can get the turtle
eat. Of course, I use
ore sherry in it than the
cipe calls for – this is the
se where more is better!

Creole Turtle Soup

4	ounces ground turtle meat, or ground chuck if turtle meat is not available
2	tablespoons butter or margarine
2	tablespoons flour
1	tablespoon chopped celery
1	tablespoon chopped yellow onions
	zest of ½ lemon, finely chopped
1	tablespoon paprika
1	teaspoon black pepper
	pinch of cayenne pepper
	pinch of oregano
	pinch of marjoram
1	teaspoon chopped parsley
	pinch of basil
4	cups beef stock, or water with beef base
1	tablespoon chopped spinach
¼	boiled egg, chopped
1	ounce dry sherry

Brown ground meat in a skillet. In a separate saucepan,
melt butter. Blend in flour and cook and stir until roux is
light brown. Add celery, onions, lemon zest, paprika, black
pepper, cayenne pepper, oregano, marjoram, parsley and
basil. Add beef stock and ground meat. Simmer 45 minutes. Add spinach, egg and sherry.

Cold Cucumber Soup with Crab

2	hard-boiled egg yolks
2	tablespoons rice vinegar
1	cup sour cream
2	seedless cucumbers, chilled (about 2 pounds)
⅓	cup fresh mint leaves
1	cup chilled buttermilk
	salt and pepper to taste
½	teaspoon extra-virgin olive oil
1	teaspoon rice vinegar
8	ounces lump crabmeat
2	tablespoons finely chopped green onions

In a bowl, mash egg yolks with 2 tablespoons vinegar to make a paste. Stir in sour cream until smooth. Peel cucumbers and halve lengthwise. Core and cut cucumber into ½-inch pieces. Place cucumber in a blender along with mint, buttermilk and salt and pepper. Purée until smooth. Whisk puréed mixture in a stream into sour cream mixture. Refrigerate. Just before serving, combine olive oil, 1 teaspoon vinegar and salt and pepper to taste. Add crabmeat and toss. Ladle cucumber mixture into soup bowls. Put a mound of crabmeat mixture in center of each bowl. Sprinkle a small amount of green onions over each serving. Serves 4.

This is definitely not Cajun, however it is really tasty and enjoyed by this Cajun. It is good to serve as an appetizer or a very refreshing meal in summer. I first was introduced to this a few years ago.

Chicken-Okra Gumbo

1	chicken fryer or hen, cut into pieces
	salt and pepper to taste
	Louisiana red pepper sauce to taste
¼	cup oil
2½	pounds fresh okra, cut into ¼-inch pieces, or 2 (16 ounce) cans
2	medium onions, chopped
¼	cup oil
1	quart water

Season chicken with salt, pepper and pepper sauce. Brown chicken in ¼ cup hot oil. Meanwhile, in another pot, sauté okra and onions in ¼ cup oil until okra has cooked down and isn't slimy. Add sautéed vegetables to chicken and season to taste. Pour in water and stir well. Cook 1 hour or until chicken is tender. Serve over cooked rice. Serves 6.

Creamy Broccoli Soup

1	medium potato, peeled and diced
1	small onion, chopped
1	14½ ounce can chicken broth
1	10 ounce package frozen chopped broccoli
1	cup milk
¼	teaspoon salt
¼	teaspoon black pepper

Combine potato, onion and broth in a saucepan. Bring to a boil over high heat. Reduce heat to low and cover. Simmer 10 minutes. Add broccoli and bring to a boil over high heat. Reduce heat to low and simmer 5 minutes or until potato is tender when poked with a fork. Purée mixture, in a blender in 3 batches, until smooth. Pour mixture into a large bowl. Stir in salt and pepper. Cover and refrigerate 6 hours or until chilled.

Beef Vegetable Soup

6	beef soup bones with meat around them
3	medium carrots, sliced (optional)
4	medium potatoes, peeled and cut into chunks
1	large onion, chopped or sliced
1	large bell pepper, julienned
2	stalks celery, cut into chunks
2	medium tomatoes, peeled and chopped
	salt and pepper to taste
	Louisiana red pepper sauce to taste

Combine all ingredients in a large stockpot. Add enough water to cover all. Bring to a boil over medium heat. Cook 2 hours or until meat is tender. Serve over rice.

Carrot Soup

1	tablespoon vegetable oil
1	medium onion, chopped
1½	16 ounce packages carrots, peeled and cut into 2 inch chunks
2	14½ ounce cans chicken broth
2	cups water
¾	teaspoon salt
¼	teaspoon ground white pepper
½	cup half-and-half
2	teaspoons chopped fresh dill

Heat oil in a 4-quart saucepan over medium heat until hot. Add onions and cook, stirring frequently, for 5 to 8 minutes or until tender and lightly browned. Add carrots, broth, water, salt and white pepper. Bring to a boil over high heat. Reduce heat to low, cover and simmer 15 minutes or until carrots are tender. Purée cooked mixture, in a blender in 3 batches, until smooth. Pour puréed mixture into a large bowl. Cover and refrigerate 6 hours or until well chilled.

To serve, stir in half-and-half and chopped dill.

hat a delightful treat
is is! I was so anxious
eat this when I visited
y friend Carl in Dallas.
e is an excellent cook
d always surprises me
ith new dishes.

Chilled Strawberry Soup with Balsamic Crème Fraîche à Carl

2	pounds strawberries, hulled
3	tablespoons mascarpone cheese
¾	cup vegetable stock
¼	cup maple syrup, or as needed based on sweetness of berries
¼	cup Grand Marnier
	salt and pepper to taste
6	tablespoons crème fraîche
1	tablespoon raspberry balsamic vinegar
2	tablespoons finely diced strawberries
1	tablespoon chopped basil
1	tablespoon maple syrup

Quarter strawberries, reserving 3 whole berries for garnish. Place quartered strawberries, cheese, vegetable stock and ¼ cup maple syrup in a blender. Purée until smooth.

Heat an empty saucepan over high heat. Remove from heat and pour in Grand Marnier. Carefully return to heat and ignite to burn off alcohol. Stir Grand Marnier into puréed soup. Season with salt and pepper. Refrigerate overnight.

Combine crème fraîche and vinegar. Dice remaining 3 whole strawberries. Mix diced berries with basil and 1 tablespoon maple syrup. To serve, spoon chilled soup into bowls. Add a dollop of crème fraîche mixture to center of each serving. Sprinkle diced strawberries over crème fraîche. Enjoy!

Crème Fraîche

¼	cup heavy cream
¼	cup sour cream

Whip heavy cream and sour cream together. Cover with plastic wrap and allow to stand at room temperature for 2 to 5 hours or until thickened. Once thickened, store in refrigerator for up to 48 hours. Stir before using.

Peachy Melon Soup

1   large cantaloupe, chilled
1   cup peach nectar
2   tablespoons lemon juice
      lime or lemon slices for garnish

Cut cantaloupe in half and scoop out and discard seeds.
Cut away rind and cut cantaloupe into bite-size pieces.
Purée cantaloupe pieces, peach nectar and lemon juice in
a blender for 1 minute or until smooth. Serve immediately, or pour into a large bowl, cover and refrigerate up
to 1 day. Garnish each serving with a slice of lime or lemon.

Creamy Artichoke & Oyster Soup

2   cups artichoke hearts
12   oysters, drained, saving juice
4   tablespoons butter, melted
4   tablespoons flour
1   cup milk
½   cup green onions, chopped fine
1   clove garlic, chopped or minced
¼   cup parsley, chopped
1   cup heavy cream
      salt and pepper to taste
¼   cup dry white wine

Reserve 4 artichoke hearts for garnish; cut in 4 pieces and
set aside.

Buzz the rest of the artichokes in blender with their
liquid. Set aside.

Make a white roux with the butter and flour. Stir in
artichoke purée, the liquid from the oysters and the milk.
Simmer with garlic, green onions and parsley. Season. Add
oysters and cook about 10 minutes or just until oysters
curl around the edges. Stir in wine and serve immediately.
Add the reserved artichokes for garnish. Serves 2.

My mama never cooked
artichokes; she would
never have made soup
with oysters. In the past
year, I have eaten this new
dish and thoroughly en-
joyed it. The combination
of oysters and artichokes
is so tasty!

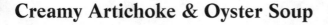

BEEF

Everyone has heard the question "Where's the beef?" Well, here is where it's at! Deb Morrell showed me and also let me sample a delicious T-Bone, my favorite cut, of course.

This is definitely not Cajun cooking from my grandmother's kitchen. I learned to serve this to my family when we first moved to Northeast Louisiana. What a change! Sometimes I would use some beef cubed steaks.

This is what Mama always ended up doing with leftover rice dressing. It was delicious and tasted even better once baked in a bell pepper. I use this as a meal!

Beef Stroganoff

4	slices bacon, chopped
2	medium onions, chopped
1	medium bell pepper, chopped
1½	pounds lean ground beef
1	4 ounce can mushrooms, sliced
	salt and pepper to taste
¼	cup water
1	cup sour cream

Cook bacon, onions and bell pepper in a pot until tender. Remove bacon and vegetables from pot and set aside, reserving bacon grease in pot. Brown beef in bacon grease. Add mushrooms and cooked bacon and vegetables to pot. Season with salt and pepper. Add water and cook 15 minutes. Stir in sour cream and cook just until hot—don't boil! Serve over rice.

Stuffed Bell Peppers

10	large bell peppers
1	pound ground beef
¼	cup oil
1	large onion, chopped
1	large bell pepper, chopped
	salt and pepper to taste
¼	cup chopped green onion tops
2	cups cooked and cooled rice

Cut off and reserve the top of 10 bell peppers; remove stems and seeds. Brown beef in oil in a skillet. Add onions and chopped bell pepper and cook about 10 minutes. Season with salt and pepper. Add green onions and mix thoroughly. Mix in rice. Stuff mixture into bell peppers and replace tops. Place stuffed peppers into a shallow baking pan and add a small amount of water to the bottom of the pan. Bake at 350 degrees for 30 minutes.

Beef Tender in Three Mustard Sauce

¼	cup olive oil
4-5	pounds beef tender
	dry mustard to taste
	salt to taste
⅓	teaspoon black pepper
⅓	cup tarragon mustard
⅓	cup Dijon mustard
¼	cup yellow mustard
⅓	teaspoon dry mustard
½	cup heavy whipping cream
3	large shallots, finely chopped

Place olive oil in the middle of a roasting pan. Lay beef on the oil and turn until beef is well coated with oil. Sprinkle liberally with dry mustard. Season lightly with salt and sprinkle top with black pepper. Bake at 450 degrees for about 35 to 45 minutes.

Meanwhile, in a mixing bowl, combine tarragon, Dijon and yellow mustards. Add ⅓ teaspoon dry mustard and mix until smooth. Whisk in cream until well blended. Set sauce aside.

After baking 35 to 40 minutes, remove beef from oven and pour mustard sauce over top. Sprinkle shallots on top. (Shallots, not green onion tops!) Return to oven and roast about 7 to 10 minutes longer or until beef is done to desired taste — you want beef pink in the middle when served. Remove beef from pan and set aside to rest. Use a whisk to blend meat drippings and mustard sauce in the pan. Thinly slice beef and arrange on a platter. Drizzle sauce on top. Enjoy!

I met a lovely lady fror Houston. She had bee watching my show an decided to e-mail me Needless to say, we ar now close friends. An now Melissa is Che Melissa. She claims I in spired her to go to culi nary school. I am rea proud of her!

Mitty Mitty's Meatloaf

was never able to cook a
ood meatloaf. However,
Melissa is great at it. She
hared her recipe and
ooked this for me often.

2	pounds ground beef
	salt and pepper to taste
	Louisiana red pepper sauce to taste
	Cajun seasoning to taste
¾	cup finely chopped onions
¾	cup finely chopped bell pepper
1	egg
⅓	cup Italian breadcrumbs
1	6 ounce can tomato paste
1	15 ounce can tomato sauce

Season ground beef with salt, pepper, pepper sauce and
Cajun seasoning. Add onions, bell pepper and egg and
mix well. Add breadcrumbs and mix well. Form mixture
into a loaf shape in a 9x13 inch foil-lined baking pan. Cover
loaf completely with tomato paste and pour tomato sauce
over the top. Cover with foil. Bake at 350 degrees for
1 hour, basting about every 15 minutes with the tomato
sauce in the pan.

Roast Beef Hash

was always puzzled
about what to do with the
eftover beef roast (or any
other type of left over
roast, etc.) after we were
ired of eating beef sand-
wiches. Well, I decided to
out together this hash. (I
ad seen my mother-in-
aw cook this several
imes.) A great way to
ransfer leftovers into a
new, tasty meal.

¼	cup oil
2	pounds leftover beef hash, cut up
1	medium onion, chopped
2	cups diced potatoes
1	cup chopped green onions
¼	cup water (optional)
	salt and pepper to taste
	Louisiana red pepper sauce to taste

Heat oil in a pot. Add beef and brown slightly. Add
onions and potatoes and cook about 20 minutes or until
potatoes are done. Add green onions and mix well. If you
would like this mixture juicy, simply add ¼ cup water
and cover. Simmer 10 minutes. Season with salt, pepper
and pepper sauce. Serve over rice.

Meat Rub

For baking a beef roast, beef ribs or chicken.

½   cup cider vinegar
½   cup white vinegar
1   teaspoon red pepper flakes
1   cup brown sugar

Combine vinegars, pepper flakes and brown sugar to make a sauce. Coat meat of choice with sauce. Bake at 350 degrees, basting every 30 minutes. For beef roast, bake 23 to 25 minutes per pound for rare, 27 to 30 minutes per pound for medium. Remove from oven and cover for about 15 minutes before carving.

This is another recip
from my dear friend
Chef Melissa. She told m
how tasty the inside of a
roast prepared in this
manner is. And she wasn'
kidding — it is delicious

Hamburger Steak

1   pound ground beef or deer
1   cup breadcrumbs
     salt and pepper to taste
     Louisiana red pepper sauce to taste
½   cup chopped onions
1   egg
     oil
2   tablespoons flour
½   cup water or milk
2   small onion, sliced

Mix together ground meat, breadcrumbs, salt, pepper, pepper sauce, onions and egg. Form mixture into oblong-shaped hamburger patties. Add oil to a skillet to cover the bottom and heat. Brown hamburger patties on both sides in oil. Remove patties, reserving pan drippings in skillet. Add flour to drippings and stir until blended. Add water and season with salt and pepper. Stir well until mixture forms a smooth gravy. Add hamburger patties back into skillet along with onion slices. Cover and cook until done, adding more water if necessary while cooking.

This is a great dish to
serve and easy to cook. I
like to use milk for my
gravy, but it is optional.
Mama would never use
milk in a gravy but I have
a tendency to change the
trend.

This is my favorite lasagne recipe. A friend, Mrs. D.C. Clark, shared it with me. It takes a long time to prepare, but is worth the wait!

To shorten the preparation, you may use the lasagne noodles raw. This is a new way that has been introduced. Also, you may use cottage cheese instead of the other cheeses.

Lasagne

	oil
2	pounds ground beef
1	stick margarine, melted
2	large onions, chopped
1	28 ounce can tomato sauce, or one 6 ounce can tomato paste
2	packages dry Italian style spaghetti sauce mix with mushrooms
3	tablespoons minced parsley
1	tablespoon garlic powder
1	tablespoon salt
2	tablespoons sugar
1	tablespoon dried sweet pepper flakes, or 1 small bell pepper, chopped
1	1 pound box lasagne noodles
1	pound Cheddar cheese, shredded
1	pound natural Swiss cheese, sliced and cut into small strips

Add oil to a skillet to cover the bottom. Brown ground beef in oil. Add margarine and onions and cook until onions are browned. Add tomato sauce plus a tomato sauce can of water. (If using tomato paste, add 2 tomato paste cans of water.) Stir in spaghetti sauce mix, fresh parsley, garlic powder, salt, sugar and pepper flakes. Cover and cook on low for 2 hours, stirring every few minutes. Cook lasagne noodles until half done; rinse.

To assemble, spray a 9x13 inch baking pan with Pam. Layer noodles, meat sauce and Cheddar and Swiss cheeses in pan. Repeat layers until pan is three-fourths full. Spoon remaining sauce on top and help it work its way through to the bottom. Bake at 325 degrees for 1 hour, 15 minutes. Serves 6 to 8.

Eggplant Dressing

1	pound ground beef
2	tablespoons oil
1	large onion, chopped
¾	cup chopped bell pepper
4	medium eggplants, peeled and chopped
1	cup water, divided
	salt and pepper to taste
	Louisiana red pepper sauce to taste
3	cups cooked and cooled rice

Brown beef in oil. Add onions, bell pepper, eggplant and some of the water. Season with salt, pepper and pepper sauce. Mix well. Cook on medium until eggplant is thoroughly mashed, adding remainder of water as needed to make moist. Add rice and mix well. Serves 4 to 6.

Mama taught me how to make a delicious rice dressing. Later on, she added the eggplant to it. I really enjoy eating it. This dish goes with any meat.

Veal New Orleans

24	ounces veal, thinly sliced
1	tablespoon flour
2	tablespoons butter or margarine
4	artichoke hearts or bottoms, drained and quartered
4	ounces sliced mushrooms, drained
2	tablespoons chopped green onions
1	tablespoon chopped parsley
1	ounce white wine
¼	cup half-and-half
	salt and coarse ground black pepper to taste

Mix veal and flour. Melt butter in a hot skillet. Add veal, stir and brown lightly. Add artichokes and mushrooms. Simmer for a couple minutes. Reduce heat to low and add green onions, parsley and wine. Mix well. Remove from heat. Add half-and-half. (Do not cook after half-and-half is added.) Season to taste with salt and pepper. Serves 4.

This is another great beef (veal) dish which Chef Hans has prepared often. He handed down many good recipes to me that he learned to cook while training under Chef Paul Prudhomme.

Mama never cooked chili at home—we ate it, but it was always in restaurants and only in the wintertime. Daddy did not like it so I guess that's why she didn't bother to cook any. But I have made it often because my children really liked it. I like it myself but without the beans.

I often cook corned beef n' cabbage even though it is not a Cajun meal. It is so easy to prepare — a meal in one pot. And it is so good and also good for you!

Chili

2	pounds ground beef
2	tablespoons oil
1	cup chopped onions
¾	cup chopped bell pepper
3	cloves garlic, chopped
1	8 ounce can tomato sauce
1	6 ounce can tomato paste
3	tablespoons chili powder
1	16 ounce can kidney beans (optional)
2	cups water or as needed
	salt and pepper to taste

Brown ground beef in hot oil. Add onions, bell pepper and garlic and cook about 10 minutes. Add tomato sauce, tomato paste, chili powder and kidney beans, if desired. Mix well and cook over low heat for about 1 hour, adding small amounts of water occasionally until done. Add enough water to reach desired thickness. Season with salt and pepper.

Corned Beef N' Cabbage

1	3 pound corned beef brisket
1	head cabbage, quartered
½	pound red potatoes, peeled and quartered
1	large onion, sliced
1	16 ounce package whole baby carrots
2	medium bell peppers, sliced
2	stalks celery, thickly sliced

Place beef along with contents of package that came with beef in a large pot. Add cabbage, potatoes, onions, carrots, bell pepper and celery. Cover all with water and bring to a boil. Boil slowly for 2½ to 3 hours or until beef is tender. Remove beef from pot, slice and arrange on a platter. Remove vegetables from pot with a large slotted spoon and arrange next to beef on platter, or serve in a bowl on the side. Serve with a good hot mustard to spread on beef as you eat it. Serves 6.

Porcupine Meatballs

1   **pound ground beef**
½   **cup dry long grain rice**
¼   **cup finely chopped onions**
        salt and pepper to taste
½   **cup flour**
½   **cup oil**
2   **cups water or as needed**

Combine ground beef, rice, onions, salt and pepper. Shape mixture into medium-sized balls. Set aside.

Brown flour in oil to make a dark roux. Add enough water to make a gravy. Bring to a boil. Drop meatballs into gravy and cook slowly for 1 hour, turning meatballs halfway through. Make sure meatballs are almost completely submerged in gravy so rice can cook.

I had never heard of these until I moved to Jones. My good friend and neighbor, Mavis Mitchel, cooked these and brought us some to eat. I was relieved when I discovered that there was no porcupine in the dish.

Smothered Beef Tongue

¼   **cup oil**
1   **large beef tongue, dressed**
1   **large onion, chopped or sliced**
4   **cups water, divided**
        salt and pepper to taste

Heat oil in a skillet. Add tongue and brown on both sides. Continue to cook until partially cooked. Add onions and 2 cups of water. Season with salt and pepper. Cover and cook on medium-high until tongue is tender, adding remainder of water as needed to cook tongue completely. It should make a brown natural gravy. Slice and serve over rice.

This was a common dish at my house. Mama would clean the tongue once the slaughter house had butchered our calves. She cooked it as above or would boil the dressed tongue until it got tender, cut it up into pieces and put it in a jar filled with clear vinegar. I enjoyed it either way. So I smothered a beef tongue for James Jones, my favorite painter, one day. He loved it—but his wife wouldn't kiss him for a whole month after he ate it.

PORK

This is the lil' piggy that stayed home! He is so cute! Angelo Piazzo toured me around his pig farm then I enjoyed a delicious *couchon de lait,* an occasion that is deeply of Cajun origin. (Angelo is the king of *couchon de lait* cooks.)

Mama could really cook these. She would sometimes brown these in a pot on the stove also then finish cooking them in the oven. We ate a lot of pork because we raised our own hogs and butchered them also. She must have learned from her brother, Bill, as he was a good cook and had a meat shop in Kaplan for a long time!

Stuffed Pork Chops

6	pork chops, each 1½ inches thick
	salt and pepper to taste
	Louisiana red pepper sauce to taste
4	tablespoons butter
1	small onion, finely chopped
¼	cup finely chopped green onion tops
1	small bell pepper, finely chopped
3	cloves garlic, finely chopped
4	slices bread
¼	cup milk

Cut slits horizontally in chops to make pockets. Season with salt, pepper and pepper sauce. Set aside. Melt butter in a saucepan. Add onions, onion tops, bell pepper and garlic and sauté until softened. Season to taste. Soak bread in milk and squeeze out. Add bread to sautéed vegetables and mix well. Stuff mixture into pockets of chops. Lay chops side by side in a pan sprayed with Pam and cover pan. Bake at 350 degrees for 1½ hours, turning chops once halfway through. Uncover and bake 30 minutes longer.

Grandma Dufour's Christmas Stuffing

2	small boxes chicken gizzards liver and gizzard of a turkey
1	pound ground pork
2	onions, minced
2	bunches green onions, white part only, finely chopped
2	stalks celery, finely chopped
2	teaspoons chopped parsley
1	tablespoon oil
3	cups cooked rice
3	cups crumbled cornbread
3	dozen fresh oysters, drained and finely chopped
1	cup chopped pecans
1	tablespoon butter, melted
2	eggs, beaten
1	teaspoon salt
½	teaspoon black pepper
6	chicken bouillon cubes, mixed with water to make broth

Cook chicken and turkey gizzards and turkey liver in boiling water until tender. Drain, reserving broth. Chop or grind gizzards and liver (ground is best). Brown pork, onions, green onions, celery and parsley in oil. Mix in rice and cornbread. Add liquid if mixture is too dry. Stir in oysters, pecans and butter. Mix in eggs, salt and pepper. Cook, stirring constantly, until eggs are cooked and stuffing can be handled easily. If stuffing is too dry, add broth, a little at a time. Stuff mixture into turkey. Cook and enjoy.

I put lots of celery and onions in boiling water with gizzards.

A dear friend of mine, Mr. Duffy Dufore, sent this recipe for me to try. It is definitely a keeper! His grandmother was a real good cook as all French ladies are! He is a good cook also; he has even cooked for Vice-President Gore and his family.

I first remember making boudin when I was about five years old. My parents used cut cow horns to stuff the casing with because there were no sausage stuffers in those days. I bothered my parents to help make boudin so badly that my father made a special little horn for me to use. (I still have it in my possession.) But then I grew older and the boudin making days became more like work than play. I knew that my parents made the best boudin in the world.

Boudin

1	pig's head, split in half, discard the eyes, nose and ears
1	6 pound pork roast
2	cups chopped onions
2	large bunches green onions, chopped
1	bunch parsley, chopped
	salt and pepper to taste
10	cups cooked rice, chilled if possible
	sausage casings, washed well
1	gallon water

Cook all pork in boiling water for 1½ hours until tender. Drain meat, reserving broth. Discard skin and remove meat from bones. Grind all meat into a very large container. Add onions, green onions and parsley. Season with salt and pepper. Add 1½ cups reserved broth or enough to make mixture real moist. If mixture becomes too dry at any time, add more broth. Add cooked rice and mix well. Stuff mixture into casings using a sausage maker. Tie ends of casings.

When ready to eat, bring 1 gallon water to a boil in a large pot. Remove from heat and add boudin, being sure boudin is fully submerged in water. Cover pot and allow to cook 10 minutes. Serve hot or cold.

To freeze boudin, put in water and allow to freeze that way as it will retain its taste better. Completely thaw to cook. This recipe makes a lot of boudin because it is not a dish that you would prepare only small portions of.

When I have any leftover boudin from a meal, I fry it in a covered skillet with some hot oil in it - enough to cover the bottom of the pot. This is also very good.

Boudin Balls

2   **pounds boudin**
2   **eggs, beaten**
     breadcrumbs
     salt and pepper to taste
     oil for frying

Remove boudin from casing and shape into small round balls. Dip balls in eggs and then roll in breadcrumbs seasoned with salt and pepper. Drop balls into hot oil and fry until golden brown, or bake at 350 degrees for 15 minutes. Serve as an appetizer.

We definitely did not have boudin balls as I grew up. All we had was the stuffing in the casing.

Ham Loaf

2   **pounds smoked ham, ground**
1   **large green bell pepper, finely chopped**
1   **medium onion, finely chopped**
     salt and pepper to taste
3   **eggs**
2   **cups milk**
3   **cups cracker crumbs**

Mix together ham, bell pepper, onions and salt and pepper. Beat together eggs and milk well. Add egg mixture to cracker crumbs and mix well. Let soak 5 minutes. Add cracker mixture to ham mixture. Shape mixture into loaves and place in loaf pans. Cover with foil. Bake at 325 degrees for 1 hour. Remove foil and baste well with pan drippings. Bake, uncovered, 2 hours longer. Serve with sauce, if desired.

Sauce (optional)

½   **pint heavy whipping cream**
¾   **jar hot horseradish**
     juice of ½ lemon

To make sauce, whip cream until it forms peaks but is not too stiff. Add horseradish and lemon juice. Chill.

A friend from Wilmot, Arkansas served this a long time ago. This is a great recipe to use up leftover ham. Sharon Farris, my friend, is a real good cook and she shared this recipe with me. This is a great dish to use up leftover ham from the holidays or a party.

I recently had the honor and privilege to visit Natchitoches and actually see Mr. Jimmy Le Zionne make these in his restaurant. He has been in business for a mighty long time and has sold many pies. They used to sell for 10 cents and now they sell for 92 cents — you call that inflation, I guess. Whatever it is, they are delicious. This is my own version of making the pies.

Natchitoches' Famous Pies

Filling

1	pound ground beef
1	pound ground pork
2	cups ground onions
1	cup ground bell pepper
¾	cup ground celery
2	cloves garlic, crushed
1	cup chopped green onion tops
	salt and pepper to taste
2	tablespoons flour

Spray the bottom of a pot with Pam. Brown ground meats in pot over medium-high heat. Add onions, bell pepper, celery and garlic and cook until done. Add onion tops and season with salt and pepper. Mix in flour. Cook about 5 minutes. Cool well.

Dough

4	cups flour
¾	cup shortening
2	eggs
	milk

To make dough, cut together flour and shortening with a pastry blender. Add eggs and mix well. Add milk, a little at a time, until a stiff dough forms. Roll out dough thin and cut into 5½-inch circles (about the size of small saucers.) Add about 1½ tablespoons of filling to the center of each circle and fold in half. Crimp edges together, making sure edges are sealed well. Bake at 425 degrees until brown, or deep fry in hot oil until they float and are golden brown. Remove and drain.

Southern Bar-B-Que

1	liter Coke
1	liter pineapple juice
1	cup brown sugar
1	rack baby pork ribs

Bar-B-Que Sauce

2	large onions, finely chopped
2	cloves garlic, finely chopped
1	small bell pepper, finely chopped
1	8 ounce can tomato paste
2	tablespoons cooking oil
2	tablespoons Worcestershire sauce
1	tablespoon dry mustard
1	cup vinegar
½	cup lemon juice
1	36 ounce bottle ketchup

Bring Coke, juice and sugar to a boil in a pot. Add ribs. Add water to pot, if needed, to be sure ribs are fully submerged in liquid. Boil 1 hour. Drain ribs. Grill ribs on a bar-b-que pit for 10 minutes on each side. Dip ribs in bar-b-que sauce and return to pit for 5 to 10 minutes longer. Enjoy!

To make sauce, combine all sauce ingredients in a large pot. Cook over medium heat, stirring occasionally, for 2 hours or until sauce thickens. If you like it sweeter, add more brown sugar to the sauce.

Classic CAJUN DEUX

Mama's bar-b-que sauce was the best. She'd make a huge pot and keep the amount she needed, then refrigerate the rest. We ate a lot of bar-b-que — that was the one meal Daddy was good at. He did use chicken quarters instead of pork for variation.

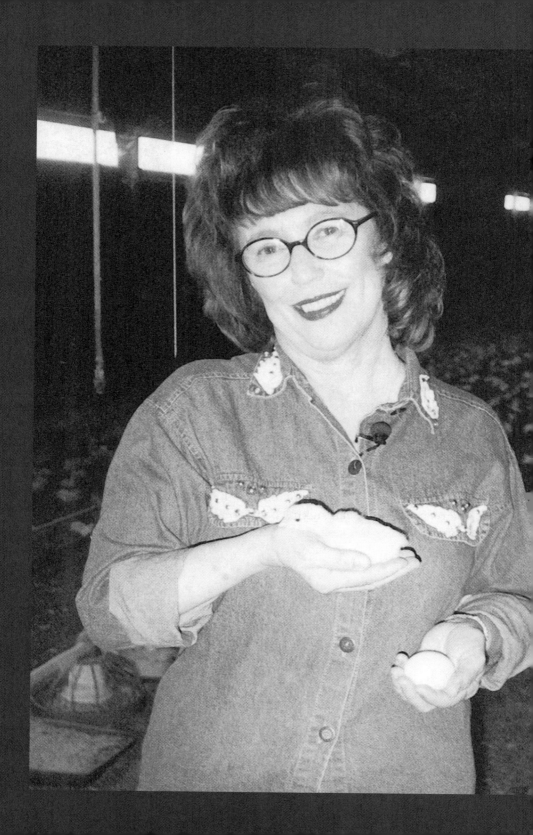

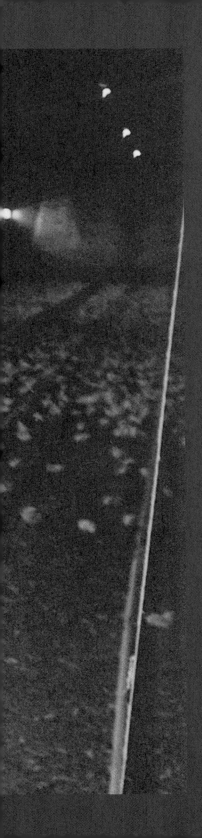

POULTRY

Chicken gumbo, sauce piquant, dumplings, fricassee and chicken stew are just a few of the many Cajun dishes that are favorites.

Of course, every home had a chicken yard. Usually, the Cajun alarm clock was the rooster crowing in the yard. One of the chores that the Cajun children have is to pick the eggs out of the nests.

This was always a favorite of Mama and Daddy's. Of course, we always had ducks in our freezer. Gueydan is the Duck Capital of America so Daddy took advantage of many hunts. Thank goodness he would clean them!

I am so glad I was finally introduced to quail. And I even found a quail farm near where I live. Now, I make sure I keep quail in my freezer year round.

Duck à Gueydan

1	cup flour
1	cup oil
1	gallon water
2	medium-size ducks, cut into serving pieces
1	large onion, chopped
1	large bell pepper, chopped
	salt and pepper to taste
	Louisiana red pepper sauce to taste
1½	cups chopped green onion tops

Cook flour in oil in a large pot to make a dark brown roux. Use a whisk to slowly blend in water. Add duck pieces, onions and bell pepper. Season with salt, pepper and pepper sauce. Boil over medium heat for 2 to 3 hours or until duck is tender. Add green onions and cook 5 minutes longer. Serve over rice. Serves 6.

Sauced Quail

6	quail, dressed
	salt and pepper to taste
1	stick butter
½	cup chopped onions
¼	cup chopped bell pepper
6	fresh mushrooms, sliced
½	cup water
1	cup white wine

Season quail with salt and pepper. Melt butter in a skillet. Add quail and brown on both sides. Remove quail from skillet and transfer to a casserole dish, breast-side up. Add onions, bell pepper and mushrooms to skillet and sauté. Add water and bring to a boil, scraping up browned bits from bottom of skillet. Add vegetable mixture to quail. Pour wine over top. Cover and bake at 350 degrees for 45 minutes. Serves 6.

Fried Turkey

1   turkey
      oil for deep frying

Marinade

1   cup warm water
1   16 ounce bottle Italian dressing
2   tablespoons lemon pepper
2   tablespoons garlic powder
2   tablespoons SeasonAll
2   tablespoons Louisiana red pepper sauce
¼   cup Worcestershire sauce
2   sticks butter, melted
      salt and pepper to taste

Prepare turkey as for baking.

Combine all marinade ingredients and strain. Pour marinade into a Cajun injector or a large veterinary syringe. Inject marinade into turkey in several areas of the breast and leg area. Cover turkey and refrigerate at least 24 hours.

Deep fry turkey in 325 to 350 degree oil, cooking 3½ minutes per pound. When done, immediately remove from oil and season with salt and pepper. Allow to stand 10 minutes before carving.

You can use peanut oil, hog lard or canola oil for deep frying. Peanut oil may be used more than once.

Smothered Quail

8   quail, dressed
      salt and pepper to taste
      Louisiana red pepper sauce to taste
½   cup oil
2   medium onions, chopped
½   cup water

Season quail with salt, pepper and pepper sauce. Brown quail in oil. Add onions and sauté. Add water and simmer over low heat for about 45 minutes or until tender. Serves 8.

My parents never fried turkey. But now it is a common way to cook turkey. The proper way is to deep fat fry it—there are turkey cookers available in most Sam's or Wal-Mart stores and also in kitchen specialty stores. They have special baskets and lifters which makes it easier. Usually it takes 5 gallons of oil. Chef Hans, my friend, taught me to not season the outside of the turkey until after it is cooked—it helps the skin to be crisp and saves the grease! Instead of a turkey, I have used the same concept with a fryer or Cornish hen which I easily fried on the stove.

Quail with Lemon Butter

1   stick butter or margarine, melted
¼   cup lemon juice
6   quail, dressed
     salt and pepper to taste
     Louisiana red pepper sauce to taste
     strips of bacon

Combine melted butter and lemon juice. Brush butter mixture over inside and outside of quail. Season with salt, pepper and pepper sauce. Wrap each quail with strips of bacon. Place quail in a baking pan and cover with foil. Bake at 350 degrees for about 1 hour, basting occasionally with remaining lemon-butter mixture. Uncover and bake 15 minutes longer or until brown. Serves 6.

I had not eaten quail until I moved to North Louisiana. (There were no quail nor quail farms in South Louisiana.) But with a nearby quail farm, I enjoy some every chance I can. My favorite way to cook quail is fried as in the following recipe.

Fried Quail

4   quail, dressed and quartered
     salt and pepper to taste
3   eggs, beaten
2   cups flour
½   cup oil

Season quail with salt and pepper. Dip quail in eggs, then dredge in flour, coating well. Fry quail in hot oil until well browned on both sides. Remove from oil and arrange on a bed of rice. Serves 8.

Wild Duck with Turnips

1   large wild duck, dressed and cut into serving pieces
2   tablespoons oil
1   large onion, chopped
2   large turnips, peeled and diced
      salt and pepper to taste

Brown duck in hot oil. Add onions and turnips. Season with salt and pepper. Smother all together, adding dabs of water until duck is tender. Serve over rice. Serves 4.

Valpatta
(Chicken N' Noodle Casserole)

4   chicken breasts
1   16 ounce bag egg noodles
1   medium onion, chopped
1   medium bell pepper, chopped
1   stick butter or margarine
1   10 ounce can mild Rotel tomatoes
1   10¾ ounce can condensed cream of mushroom soup
1   10¾ ounce can condensed cream of chicken soup
      salt and pepper to taste
1   8 ounce package Velveeta cheese, shredded

Cook chicken in a saucepan of boiling water until done. Remove chicken and set aside to cool, reserving broth in saucepan. Cook noodles in broth; drain. Debone chicken and cut into chunks. Sauté onions and bell peppers in butter. Add tomatoes, soups, chicken chunks and noodles. Mix well and season with salt and pepper. Add cheese and mix thoroughly. Bake at 375 degrees for 20 to 25 minutes. Serve hot. If preparing ahead, refrigerate up to 2 days or freeze before baking.

Crawfish may be substituted for chicken - just sauté 1 pound of crawfish tailmeat with onions and bell pepper and continue as above.

I really do not like turnips but I found out to my surprise that I do like this dish very much! The duck gives the turnips a wonderful flavor and vice versa. Mama had access to a lot of ducks and, of course, we had a turnip patch, too.

A young lady friend, Nancy, introduced me to this great dish! It is simply delicious yet so easy. A green salad is all that is necessary to serve with this.

Chicken à Jodie

2	tablespoons oil
1	large fryer, cut into serving pieces
1	cup chopped onions
½	cup chopped bell pepper
¼	cup chopped celery
3	cloves garlic, chopped
1	quart tomato juice
	salt and pepper to taste
	Louisiana red pepper sauce to taste

Heat oil in a pot over medium-high heat. Add chicken
pieces and brown. Remove chicken from pot. Add onions, bell pepper, celery and garlic and sauté until limp.
Add tomato juice and stir, scraping up brown bits from
bottom of pot. Return chicken to pot. Season with salt,
pepper and pepper sauce. Simmer, covered, for about 20
to 30 minutes or until chicken is cooked and sauce in thickened. If sauce is too thin when chicken is cooked, thicken
by adding 2 tablespoons cornstarch mixed with ¼ cup cold
water and simmer 5 minutes or until thickened as desired.
Serve over rice.

Smothered Turkey Wings, Necks and Drumsticks

2	turkey wings
3	turkey necks
3	turkey drumsticks
	salt and pepper to taste
¼	cup oil
1	quart water or as needed

Season turkey wings, necks and drumsticks with salt and
pepper. Heat oil in a heavy pot. Add turkey pieces and
brown well on all sides, adding dabs of water as you brown.
Continue until turkey is tender, adding enough water to
form a light golden gravy. Cover and allow to stand for
10 minutes. Serve over rice.

Fried Chicken with Gravy

1   small fryer, cut into serving pieces
     salt and pepper to taste
     Louisiana red pepper sauce to taste
2   eggs, beaten
2   cups flour
¾   cup oil (approximately)
2   tablespoons flour
½   cup milk or water

Season chicken pieces with salt, pepper and pepper sauce. Dip chicken completely in eggs, then dredge in 2 cups flour, coating well. Heat oil in a skillet. Drop floured chicken in hot oil and fry until golden brown on both sides and cooked throughout. Transfer chicken to a platter. Remove most of grease from skillet. Add 2 tablespoons flour to skillet, season with salt and pepper and stir well for about 1 minute. Slowly stir in milk and blend until smooth. Cook and stir constantly until thickened as desired. Serve over rice.

I love fried chicken but often I don't have any gravy to serve over rice when I do fry chicken. So I make this gravy using milk. This is a popular gravy in North Louisiana. And this Cajun loves it.

Baked Quail

2   quail, whole and dressed
     salt and pepper to taste
     Louisiana red pepper sauce
4   slices bacon
     oil

Season quail with salt, pepper and pepper sauce. Wrap each quail with 2 bacon slices and secure with toothpicks. Cover bottom of a baking pan with oil. Place wrapped quail in pan and cover with foil. Bake at 350 degrees for 45 to 60 minutes. Uncover and bake 20 minutes longer. Serves 2.

This is a great way to cook quail. And it is so easy. Since I have access to a quail farm, I keep some in my freezer to enjoy as I desire.

DEER

This is definitely a trophy. The General will be so proud to add it to his collection. And, of course, I was happy to add it to my pot for dinner!

Melissa, my daughter, is a real good cook. She loves to experiment with new dishes. That is how she came up with this one. What a treat it was when she cooked these for me!

Deer Roll-Ups

1	pound tenderized deer steaks
	salt and pepper to taste
	Louisiana red pepper sauce to taste
1	16 ounce bottle Italian dressing
1	cup finely chopped onions
½	cup finely chopped celery
½	cup finely chopped bell pepper
2	tablespoons finely chopped garlic
3	tablespoons butter
6	strips bacon
¼	cup water

Flatten deer steaks with a rolling pin until very thin. Season with salt, pepper and pepper sauce. Place steaks in a bowl and cover with Italian dressing. Cover bowl with foil and refrigerate overnight.

Line a 9x13-inch baking dish and spray with Pam. Drain marinated meat on paper towels, pressing meat lightly into towels to remove most of the marinade. Sauté onions, celery, bell pepper and garlic in butter until vegetables are softened. Place sautéed mixture on steaks. Roll steaks lengthwise in jelly roll style. Wrap bacon slices around meat to completely cover meat and secure with toothpicks. Place wrapped meat in baking pan. Add water to pan and cover with foil. Bake at 400 degrees for 30 minutes. Remove foil and bake 10 minutes longer.

Fried Deer Steaks

1   **pound deer steaks, preferably backstrap**
       salt and pepper to taste
2   **eggs, beaten**
1   **cup flour**
       oil for frying

Pound steaks well to tenderize if they haven't already been tenderized at the processing plant. Season well with salt and pepper. Dip steaks completely in eggs, then dredge in flour until well coated. Heat oil in a skillet until very hot. Drop steaks into hot oil and fry until browned. Steaks cook quickly so don't overcook. Serve hot.

Bar-B-Qued Deer Backstrap

2   **cups red wine or red wine vinegar**
1   **cup vegetable or olive oil**
¼   **cup Worcestershire sauce**
2   **medium onions, chopped**
3   **cloves garlic, crushed**
2   **tablespoons dry mustard**
1   **4 to 5 pound venison tenderloin**
       salt and pepper to taste
       Louisiana red pepper sauce to taste

Combine wine, oil, Worcestershire sauce, onions, garlic and mustard and mix well. Season deer with salt, pepper and pepper sauce. Pour marinade over seasoned meat and refrigerate overnight.

Char venison on each side over hot (gray) coals. Continue to cook over medium-hot coals to desired degree of doneness. Remove from heat, slice and serve. Serves 8.

Fried deer steaks are a
good as chicken frie
beef steaks. I learned t
appreciate deer more a
I learned how to cook i
I even enjoy the hun
and I have an 8-poin
trophy to prove it!

We never ate deer as
grew up. My daddy wa
not a deer hunter so
guess that tells me why
But once I moved to
North Louisiana, m
husband became an avi
deer hunter. So now
have learned how to
cook venison severa
ways due to the fact tha
every year we get a new
mount on the wall! It i
not one of my favorite
dishes, however.

Venison Roast

4-5	pounds venison roast
	salt and pepper to taste
	Louisiana red pepper sauce to taste
3	tablespoons minced garlic
1	large onion, chopped
¼	cup oil
1	cup water

Season roast with salt, pepper and pepper sauce. Refrigerate overnight. Cut slits in roast. Combine garlic and onion and stuff into slits. Brown roast in hot oil on all sides. Reduce heat to medium and add dabs of water until roast is done. Before slicing and serving, add a dab of water to form a gravy. Serve hot. Serves 4 to 6.

Smothered Deer Meat à la Raymond

¾	cup oil
5	pounds tenderized deer meat, cut in pieces
	Creole seasoning to taste
2	medium onions, chopped
1	medium bell pepper, chopped
5	cups water, divided
¼	cup plus 1 tablespoon vinegar

Heat oil in a pot over high heat. Season deer meat with Creole seasoning and brown on all sides in oil. As pieces brown, remove them and add more meat until all is browned. Remove all meat. Add onions and bell pepper to drippings in pot and sauté until softened. Add meat back to pot and let mixture brown a bit more. Add 1 cup water or enough to cover meat. Stir mixture and cover pot. Cook over medium-high for about 10 minutes. Add vinegar plus enough water to cover meat again and stir. Cover and cook until meat is tender. Serve with rice.

Deer Chili

¼	cup cooking oil
1	pound deer, ground
1	pound beef, ground
½	pound pork, ground
2	large onions, chopped
3	ribs celery, chopped
1	large bell pepper, chopped
4	large cloves of garlic, chopped
2	8 ounce cans tomato sauce
2	16 ounce cans refried beans
2	ounces chili powder
¼	cup dry sherry wine
	salt and pepper to taste
	grated Cheddar cheese

Brown meats in oil. Add onions, bell pepper, celery and garlic and cook until tender. Add tomato sauce, beans and chili powder. Cook for about one hour on a low fire. Season and add wine. Cook for 10 minutes. Serves 8 to 10.

CRAWFISH & LOBSTER

Going to a crawfish boil is the main way for Cajuns (or foreigners) to entertain. Everyone has a great time visiting with family and friends. And by the look on my brother's face, he is also enjoying the most popular small crustacean, delicious Louisiana crawfish. Straight from the field into the pot, on to the table for all to enjoy!

My niece, Deborah, and I had a real good time one Sunday putting this recipe together. Being the good cook she is, she had been experimenting with this dish for some time. After making a big mess in the kitchen (all good cooks are messy cooks) we concluded with this delicious dish. After a busy morning, we sat down to enjoy our results. Naming the dish was more of a problem than preparing it!

Eggplant Crawfish Delight

1	medium eggplant
2	eggs, beaten
2	cups flour
2	cups oil
1	stick butter or margarine
1½	cups chopped onions
1½	cups chopped bell pepper
1	cup chopped celery
3	cloves garlic, chopped
1	pound crawfish tail meat
3	tablespoons white wine
¼	cup chicken broth
1	cup chopped green onion tops
	salt and pepper to taste
1	pound shredded Cheddar cheese
1½	cups Parmesan cheese
1	9-inch cornbread, crumbled, or 3 cups breadcrumbs

Peel eggplant and slice into thin rounds. Dip slices in eggs, then dredge in flour. Fry eggplant in hot oil until golden brown on both sides. Drain eggplant on paper towels.

Melt butter in a saucepan. Add onions, bell pepper, celery and garlic and sauté. Add crawfish tail meat and wine and cook 10 minutes. Add broth and green onions and season with salt and pepper.

In a large baking pan or casserole dish, layer half the fried eggplant, all the crawfish mixture, all of both cheeses and half of cornbread crumbs. Layer with remaining eggplant slices and top with remaining cornbread. Cover with foil. Bake at 350 degrees for 30 to 40 minutes. Serves 6 to 8.

Crawfish Casserole

Sauté 1 c bell pepper (chopped)
1 c celery (chopped)
1 c onion (chopped) in 1 block butter

If using raw Crawfish cook for a few minutes with the above ingredients.
1½-2 lb crawfish

Add 1 can Cream of Mushroom Soup
1 can Cheddar Cheese Soup

Add Parsley Flakes + Onion tops + pepper

Add 2 cups cooked rice mix well

Place in greased casserole. Top with crushed cornflakes or potato chips.

Bake at 350° for 20-25 minutes or until bubbly.

May be fixed then frozen and Baked later.

This was one of Mama's favorite dishes. I am so glad I found it in the file!

Busy fingers at the crawfish processing plant in Basile, Louisiana.

This is another casserole I have learned to cook and enjoy. It always comes in handy when company is coming because it is so easy to prepare and just pop into the oven. Just a plain salad and bread is all you need with this as it is so good itself.

This is always a popular dish at a wedding.

Crawfish Casserole

1	cup chopped onions
¾	cup chopped bell pepper
4	tablespoons butter or margarine
1	pound crawfish tails, peeled
1	15 ounce can corn, drained
¼	cup flour
2	eggs, beaten
¼	cup chopped green onion tops
	salt and pepper to taste

Sauté onions and bell pepper in butter. Add crawfish, corn, flour, eggs and green onions. Season with salt and pepper. Pour mixture into a casserole dish. Bake, uncovered, at 350 degrees for 25 minutes.

Crawfish Dip

1	cup chopped onions
½	cup chopped bell pepper
½	cup chopped celery
⅓	cup chopped green onion tops
⅓	cup chopped parsley
	garlic to taste
1	1 ounce jar chopped pimientos
2	teaspoons margarine
2-3	pounds crawfish or shrimp, cut in half or into thirds
3-4	10¾ ounce cans condensed cream of mushroom soup
	salt and cayenne pepper to taste

Sauté onions, bell pepper, celery, green onions, parsley, garlic and pimientos in margarine. Add crawfish and cook 1 minute. Stir in soup and cook until crawfish are fully cooked. Season with salt and cayenne pepper.

Crawfish Balls

2	pounds crawfish tails, peeled
1	medium onion, finely chopped
4	slices bread
1	egg, beaten
¼	cup finely chopped parsley
¼	cup finely chopped green onion tops
	salt and pepper to taste
1	cup plain breadcrumbs

Grind crawfish, onions and bread together. Add egg, parsley and green onions and mix thoroughly. Season with salt and pepper and mix. Shape mixture into quarter-size balls. Roll balls lightly in breadcrumbs. Bake at 350 degrees for 20 minutes. Makes about 3½ dozen.

Crawfish Fettuccine

1	onion, finely chopped
½	bell pepper, finely chopped
1	clove garlic, crushed
1	stick butter
2-3	tablespoons flour
2	tablespoons parsley flakes
2	pounds crawfish tails, peeled
1½	pounds Velveeta jalapeño cheese, shredded
⅔	cup half-and-half
1	pound dry fettucine or wide egg noodles
	Parmesan cheese

Sauté onions, bell pepper and garlic in butter. Add flour and cook and stir 5 minutes. Add parsley and crawfish. Fold in Velveeta and half-and-half. Cook on low for about 30 minutes. Cook noodles, drain and rinse. Mix noodles and cheese sauce and pour into a 9x13-inch baking dish. Sprinkle with Parmesan cheese. Bake at 350 degrees for about 20 minutes.

Crawfish Pie

1	stick butter
2	cloves garlic, chopped
½	cup chopped onions
½	cup chopped bell pepper
½	cup chopped celery
1	pound crawfish
1	12 ounce can evaporated milk
1	10¾ ounce can condensed cream of mushroom soup
	salt and pepper to taste
3	tablespoons cornstarch
¼	cup cold water
2	pie crusts, unbaked

Melt butter in a saucepan. Add garlic, onions, bell pepper and celery and sauté until tender. Add crawfish and cook 10 minutes. Stir in milk and soup and season with salt and pepper. Cook until crawfish is done. Dissolve cornstarch in cold water and add to crawfish mixture. Cook until mixture is thickened. Pour mixture into a pie crust. Top with second crust. Bake at 350 degrees for about 30 minutes or until pie crust is cooked.

Crawfish Maque Choux

1	stick butter or margarine
1	large onion, chopped (1 cup)
1	large bell pepper, chopped (1 cup)
1	pound crawfish tails, peeled
2	medium tomatoes, diced (1 cup)
1	16 ounce can whole corn, drained
1	12 ounce can creamed corn
	salt and pepper to taste

Melt butter in a skillet. Add onions, bell pepper and crawfish and sauté. Add tomatoes and both cans of corn. Season with salt and pepper. Cook on medium heat, uncovered, for about 30 minutes. Delicious served over rice or as a side dish.

Many people don't realize where crawfish come from. I don't know for sure, but my opinion is that lobsters began swimming down from Nova Scotia. By the time they reached Louisiana, they had shrunk down to the size of a crawfish! But now, I enjoy both, preferably the lobster.

My friend, Freddie, who works at Wimmer Cookbooks, was puzzled at my lobster section in my book. Little does he know that Cajuns eat lobster as well as crawfish! Crawfish are just small lobsters, anyway — they just wore down in size as they swam down the Mississippi River!

Boiled Lobster

salt
lobster
lemon wedges
melted butter

In a large kettle, bring 4 inches of water to a boil. Add a pinch of salt and bring to a full boil. Plunge lobster, head first, into boiling water. Cover and cook 15 to 20 minutes. Serve with lemon and melted butter.

Fried Lobster

1   1 pound lobster, dressed and steamed
1   egg, beaten
1   cup flour
     oil for deep frying

Cut lobster tail meat into chunks about ½-inch thick. Dip meat in egg, then dredge in flour until well coated. Drop meat into hot oil and fry until golden brown.

While traveling along the eastern coast, I ordered this dish. It was so good that I continue to cook it — buying my lobster out of a lobster tank at the nearest grocery store.

The first time I ate lobster was at Cobb's Restaurant in New Orleans. It was called Lobster Therma-dore. Later, the whole Zaunbrecher family came for a visit in Jones. The men cleaned the 5 dozen lobsters we had ordered shipped in from Massach. I was in charge of the stuffing. Linda, my sister-in-law, and I broiled all of them and sent them by tray-fulls to the camp for the others to enjoy. How-ever, we kept 4 for us to eat last but not least. Needless to say, the sup-per was a great success!

Stuffed Lobster

2	1½ to 2 pound live lobsters
1	cup finely chopped onions
1	cup finely chopped bell pepper
½	cup finely chopped celery
½	pound crabmeat
½	pound shrimp, peeled, deveined and chopped
1	stick butter or margarine
1	hamburger bun, soaked in water and squeezed
	salt and pepper to taste
	Louisiana red pepper sauce to taste
1	stick butter, melted
	juice of 2 lemons

Split live lobsters in half and wash out inside intestines. Lay lobster on side and remove claws, reserving claw meat. Leave body and tail together.

Sauté onions, bell pepper, celery, crabmeat, shrimp and reserved lobster claw meat in 1 stick butter. Add soaked and squeezed bread and mix well. Season with salt, pepper and pepper sauce. Stuff mixture into lobster cavities. Transfer lobster to a baking pan. Combine 1 stick melted butter and lemon juice. Baste lobster with lemon butter sauce. Broil lobster, basting frequently, for 5 to 10 minutes or until tail begins to curl. Remove from oven and serve immediately. Serves 2.

Broiled Lobster

1	2½ pound live lobster
4	tablespoons butter, melted
	juice of 1 lemon
4	tablespoons butter, melted

Lay lobster on its back and make a deep sharp cut through the whole length of the body and tail with a sharp knife or cutting shears. Spread open and remove the stomach. Crack claws with a cracker. Lay on a large baking dish, shell-side down. Drizzle melted butter over tail meat. Broil 15 to 20 minutes or until flesh begins to pull away from tail shell, basting frequently with butter. Combine lemon juice with 4 tablespoons melted butter to make a dipping sauce. Serve lobster hot with sauce on the side.

I just love lobster! One fall, I took a trip along the East coast, where lobster is plentiful and cheap. I ate lobster twice a day for a whole week! The best way I enjoy lobster is to fry it, but then the other ways aren't bad either. I first ate the fried tail meat on my trip — it was a shock how tasty it was!

Lobster Newburg

8	tablespoons butter
½	cup flour
2	cups half and half
2	teaspoons salt
	white pepper, to taste
	dash of cayenne pepper
½	cup sherry
4	cups cooked lobster, shrimp or crabmeat
½	cup cracker crumbs

Melt the butter and add the flour, stirring to form a paste. Combine the milk and half and half and slowly add to the above. Add the salt, white pepper, and cayenne pepper. Cook over medium heat until thickened and then add the sherry. Combine the sauce with the shellfish and pour into a 2½-quart casserole. Top with the cracker crumbs and bake at 300 degrees for 20 to 30 minutes. Serve with rice or patty shells. Serves 6 to 8

SHRIMP

Now that's what I call a large shrimp! I had a great time with Shrimp Louie and he, in return, enjoyed the delicious shrimp dish I cooked. We made a lot of friends at the Chef's Cook-Off in Metairie, Louisiana.

My day at the prawn farm was most exciting and educational. They are fun to seine and very tasty! Little did I know about prawns. My nephew, Jeff, informed me that prawns are actually only a different name for shrimp (and maybe just a little bit larger in size).

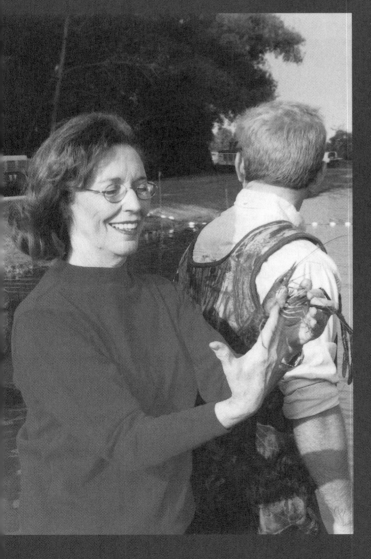

I had not eaten prawns as a young person. Last year, my nephew-in-law, Jeff, gave me a beautiful batch. I have tried cooking them different ways, but this is my favorite. Guess I'll never be too old to try something new. However, I have learned not to mistake a prawn for a shrimp — they are two different species.

I am not very fond of boiled shrimp — my favorite way to cook them is fried. But Mama often served boiled shrimp, then everybody had to peel their own. This goes well with a green salad, French bread, corn-on-the-cob and boiled potatoes. You may boil the shrimp in with the boiled corn and potatoes.

Prawns in Pasta

2	pounds medium prawns or shrimp
4	tablespoons butter or olive oil
2	cups thinly sliced fresh mushrooms
1	cup chopped green onion tops
1	pint heavy whipping cream
1	cup shredded Cheddar or Swiss cheese
	salt and pepper to taste
	cooked angel hair pasta

Sauté prawns in butter or olive oil. Add mushrooms and green onions and sauté slightly. Add cream and cheese. Heat over low heat until cheese melts. Season with salt and pepper. Serve over angel hair pasta.

Boiled Shrimp

1	gallon water
4-5	whole cloves
4	cloves garlic
2	bay leaves
	salt and pepper to taste
3	pounds shrimp, unpeeled

Combine water, cloves, garlic, bay leaves and salt and pepper in a large pot. Bring to a boil. Add shrimp and bring back to a boil. Boil 3 minutes only. Remove from heat and drain. Cover with ice to chill, or serve hot. Serves 4 to 6.

Cajun Fettuccine

12   medium shrimp, peeled and deveined
2   teaspoons minced garlic
¾   cup sliced smoked sausage
1   tablespoon olive oil
    salt and pepper to taste
2   tablespoons dry sherry
⅓   cup half-and-half
⅓   cup chicken stock
¼   cup chopped green onion tops
⅔   cup grated Parmesan cheese
3   cups cooked fettuccine

Sauté shrimp, garlic and sausage in olive oil in a pot. Season with salt and pepper. Deglaze pot by adding sherry. Add half-and-half and chicken stock and heat, but do not boil. Stir in green onions and cheese. Serve over fettuccine.

⟫ Mama's RECIPE ⟪

Hot shrimp dip
10 oz. can frozen shrimp soup
3 ½ oz. can mushrooms, chopped and drain
6 oz. roll garlic cheese, Dash Tabasco
1 Tabl. lemon juice, 4½ oz. can chop shrimp,
1 Tablespoon worcestershire sauce
Thaw shrimp soup, Place in
double boiler, add all other ingredients
Heat and serve hot.

Mama's recipe she got from a neighbor, Mae Mae.

One of my dear friends which I met through the show, is Chef Melissa Swift from Houston, Texas. She just got her Chef's hat and I am very proud of her. She loves to cook and she said I had been her biggest incentive to complete her education. This is one of her recipes which she sent to me.

This is what Chef Melissa wrote to me when she sent me the recipe:

"I began watching your show all the time. You have been the biggest incentive for me. I have learned so much that my family watches it also. I am so proud that you took the time to e-mail me. You are a true friend. I know that you give your all to people and that's what it takes to be a very special person."

She is also a very special person and great chef.

Cajun BBQ Shrimp

2	pounds medium shrimp, unpeeled
2	sticks butter
6	cloves garlic, chopped
1	tablespoon chopped fresh basil
2	teaspoons chopped fresh rosemary
¼	cup freshly squeezed lemon juice
3	tablespoons Worcestershire sauce
	salt and pepper to taste
	Louisiana red pepper sauce to taste

Mix all ingredients in a large pan. Bake at 400 degrees, stirring occasionally, until shrimp turn pink in color. Remove immediately and serve hot with French bread.

Grilled Shrimp

1	tablespoon lemon juice
1	teaspoon salt
¼	teaspoon black pepper
¼	teaspoon Creole seasoning
¼	teaspoon lemon pepper seasoning
¼	teaspoon dried dill
24	(18 to 24 count) shrimp, peeled and deveined

Combine all ingredients except shrimp. Season only one side of shrimp with seasoning mixture. Cover shrimp with plastic wrap and refrigerate 2 hours. Cook on a preheated grill for 8 minutes or until shrimp are done.

Shrimp Balls

1	pound shrimp, peeled and chopped
2	medium potatoes, boiled and mashed
1	small onion, chopped
1	small bell pepper, chopped
1	egg, beaten
	salt and pepper to taste
½	cup flour
2	tablespoons oil

Mix shrimp, mashed potatoes, onions, bell pepper, beaten egg and salt and pepper. Shape mixture into balls. Roll balls in flour and brown in hot oil in a skillet. Remove balls from skillet and serve hot.

I had never heard of shrimp balls because we always had shrimp gumbo or fried shrimp when I was growing up. But I guess I am never too old to learn new cooking methods. These are delicious and really are popular at weddings or socials.

Shrimp Au Gratin

2	pounds shrimp, peeled and chopped
4	tablespoons margarine
1½	sticks margarine
¾	cup flour
3	cups evaporated milk
4	ounces American or Cheddar cheese, shredded
2	tablespoons minced onion
¼	cup chopped green onion tops
	salt and pepper to taste

Sauté shrimp in 4 tablespoons margarine. In a separate pot, melt 1½ sticks margarine. Stir in flour. Add milk to make a white sauce. Bring to a boil. Add cheese, onions, green onions and sautéed shrimp. Season with salt and pepper. Spoon into individual baking dishes. Bake at 350 degrees for 20 to 25 minutes. Serves 8.

This dish is one I created wondering how it would compare to crabmeat or crawfish au gratin. It is different yet equally as good.

Crayfish or Shrimp Dip.
2 to 3 lbs. crayfish
3 or 4 can cream of mushroom soup
1 cup chopped onions
1/2 cup chopped Bell peppers - 1/2 cup chopped
Celery, Two third cup onion top & Parsley
1 small jar pimientos, Garlic powder
salt & red pepper - to taste. Use less
salt than usual since the Escort
Crackers, which are the only recommended
for this special Dip, will give the
required added salt flavor.
     Saute — Onions, Bell peppers,
Celery, pimientos in 2 teaspoons
margerine
Add and cook for 1 minute crayfish
that have been cut in two halves if large,
or thirds. Add mushroom soup and
cook until crayfish are fully cooked
Turn off heat, and add onion top & Parsley
Add 1/2 cup flour with water to form thick paste
                    add to Dip.

Mama loved this dip — she ate it over rice sometimes or just plain without the crackers.

Shrimp Jambalaya

1	pound shrimp, peeled and deveined
1	stick butter
½	cup chopped onions
¼	cup chopped celery
¼	cup chopped bell pepper
1	clove garlic, chopped
2	sticks butter
1	cup crabmeat
1	10¾ ounce can condensed cream of mushroom soup
½	cup chopped green onions tops
½	cup chopped parsley
¼	cup tomato sauce
	salt and pepper to taste
1	cup cooked rice

Sauté shrimp in 1 stick butter in a pot. Remove shrimp and set aside. In same pot, sauté onions, celery, bell pepper and garlic in 2 sticks butter. Add sautéed shrimp, crabmeat, soup, green onions, parsley and tomato sauce. Mix well. Season with salt and pepper. Mix in rice. Transfer mixture to a baking dish sprayed with PAM. Bake at 350 degrees for 20 minutes.

Mama had to learn how to make casseroles because she had been cooking in pots on the stove for many years. But she learned how to make delicious casseroles and loved to do that because it was so easy yet delicious with easy clean up. I found this recipe in her old recipe file box. Now I am following in her footsteps (in the kitchen.)

This type of coating for shrimp is great as it eliminates the flour mess yet gives a wonderful fried shrimp. The beer adds flavor to the batter but really cooks out so as no alcohol is present. I wasn't aware of how to cook with beer until later in years because that was not what Mama used as an ingredient.

Beer Batter Fried Shrimp

2	cups flour
	salt and pepper to taste
1	12 ounce can beer
2	dozen shrimp, peeled, deveined and butterflied
	oil for deep-frying

Season flour with salt and pepper. Pour enough beer into flour mixture to make a batter thick enough to coat shrimp. Beat until frothy. Drop shrimp into batter and coat well. Fry shrimp in hot oil for 3 to 5 minutes or until golden brown. Drain on paper towels. Serve hot.

This is my own version of shrimp étouffée. I like it because the tomato soup gives it a smooth taste. Served over a bed of rice, the cook cannot go wrong.

Shrimp Étouffée

3	pounds shrimp, peeled and deveined
1	cup chopped onions
½	cup chopped bell pepper
¼	cup chopped celery
1	stick margarine or butter
1	8 ounce can condensed tomato soup
	salt and pepper to taste
	Louisiana red pepper sauce to taste

Sauté shrimp, onions, bell pepper and celery in margarine. Add tomato soup and simmer about 30 minutes. Season with salt, pepper and pepper sauce. Serve over rice.

Shrimps
1 cup cook rice
1/2 " chopped onions
1/4 " chopped celery
1/4 " " bell pepper
1/2 " onion top & parsley
1/4 " Tomatoe sauce
1 " Crabmeat
1/2 " Deviened shrimp
1/2 Teaspoon salt
1/2 " red pepper
1/2 " Tabasco
1/2 block butter
1/2 can mushroom soup
1 pod Garlic

Bake 20 min. at 350 degre

I found Mama's handwritten recipe for "Shrimps."

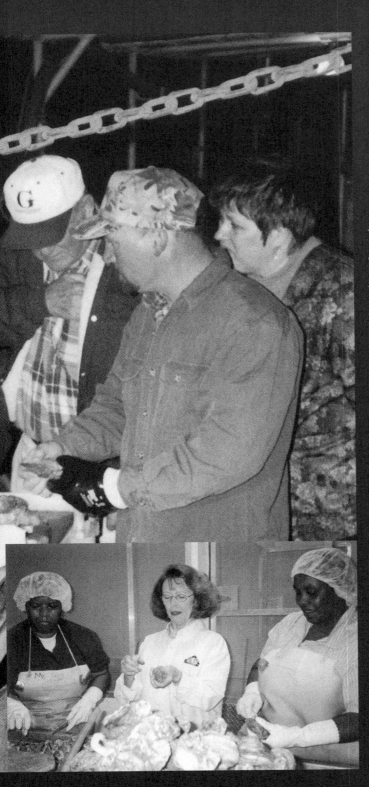

OYSTERS

Touring Motivatit Seafoods in Houma was so exciting. The oysters tasted the best I had ever had (and I ate my weight in oysters-on-the-half-shell that day!)

Recently I spent some time at my son's house in Grapevine, Texas. While visiting there, we enjoyed a wonderful meal at a quaint seafood grill, Half Shells. I was so curious about the above dish that I ordered it. And I was so glad I did — it was delicious! I got the manager, Michael Easley, to share the recipe with me. I liked it so much that I will definitely be preparing this half Mexican, half Cajun dish in my Cajun kitchen.

Oyster Nachos

6	tortilla chips
1	can chipotle peppers in adobo sauce
½	cup Tartar Sauce (recipe below)
6	oysters, drained
1	cup yellow cornmeal
	oil for deep frying
	Pico de Gallo (recipe below) for garnish

Line a plate with chips. Combine chipotle peppers and tartar sauce, according to your taste, in a food processor and mix. Dredge oysters in cornmeal to coat. Fry oysters in hot oil. Drizzle chipotle sauce mixture over chips. Lay an oyster on each chip. Sprinkle pico de gallo on chips and around plate. Serve hot.

Tartar Sauce

1	cup mayonnaise
2	tablespoons sweet pickle relish
1	small onion, grated
1	tablespoon horseradish
	salt and pepper to taste

Mix all sauce ingredients in a food processor. Refrigerate at least 30 minutes before serving.

Pico de Gallo

2	cups finely diced tomato
½	whole jalapeño, finely chopped
½	cup finely chopped red onion
2	tablespoons lemon juice
2	tablespoons lime juice
1	tablespoon finely chopped green onions
	salt and pepper to taste
½	teaspoon ground cumin

Combine all ingredients and refrigerate.

The chipotle peppers in adobo sauce comes in a can and may be found in the Mexican food section of your grocery store. However, Tabasco pepper sauce has a new chipotle pepper sauce which I prefer using. It is so much easier, better tasting and even made in Avery Island, Louisiana.

Oysters Rockefeller

4	tablespoons butter
½	cup chopped yellow onions
1	tablespoon flour
8	ounces spinach, cooked, drained and chopped
½	cup chopped parsley
½	cup oyster juice (liquor), fish stock or water
1	ounce Herbsaint or Pernod liqueur
2	anchovy fillets, chopped (optional)
	Chef Hans Creole seasoning to taste, or salt and pepper to taste
2	dozen oysters, shucked and on the half shell

Melt butter in a skillet over medium heat until almost brown. Add onions and cook 1 minute. Stir in flour and mix well. Add spinach, parsley, oyster juice, liqueur and anchovy fillets. Simmer 3 to 5 minutes — in order to maintain a nice green color, do not overcook. Allow mixture to cool before spreading over oysters. Season to taste. Spread mixture evenly over oysters. Bake at 325 degrees for 15 to 20 minutes.

Oyster Bacon Wrap-Arounds

10	strips bacon, cut in half
20	raw oysters, drained
	cornmeal
	oil for frying

Wrap a piece of bacon around each oyster and secure each with a toothpick. Coat oysters with cornmeal. Drop oysters into hot oil and fry about 5 minutes or until browned. Drain and eat hot.

I was invited to a camp supper a few years ago. Only once I arrived did I realize what was being served — oysters wrapped in bacon! Dale Ross and Vincent Zaunbrecher were the chief cooks. It was a very slow process of preparation, so I helped them. We ate as we cooked this very delicious dish served with French fries. This was a new experience for me.

A classic New Orleans creation, which is now famous the world over. There are now many variations in recipes and ingredients. There are many stories as to its origin, depending on which restaurant you go to. My friend, Chef Hans, taught me how to prepare and enjoy. He trained at Brennan's where he became "Creole-ized". He and I have exchanged a lot of recipes. Guess I am responsible for "Cajun-izing" him!

Another way to cook bacon wrapped oysters would be to broil them until the bacon is crisp.

Both of these could be used as appetizers but I prefer eating them as the main course (Cajuns don't have appetizers.)

Oysters Bienville

3	**tablespoons butter**
2	**tablespoons flour**
4-5	**chopped green onion tops**
1	**chicken bouillon cube**
	milk
1	**4 ounce can chopped mushrooms, drained**
3	**tablespoons sherry or white wine**
	salt and pepper to taste
	oysters
	breadcrumbs and paprika for sprinkling

Make a white sauce by melting butter in a saucepan. Blend in flour and cook slowly for about 2 minutes. Add green onions and sauté. Stir in bouillon cube. Add just enough milk to make a thick white sauce. Add mushrooms and sherry and season with salt and pepper. Cook slowly for 15 minutes or until thick and smooth.

Pan broil oysters in shells (which have been opened) for a few minutes to remove water. Place oysters in baking dishes and cover with sauce. Sprinkle with breadcrumbs and paprika. Bake at 350 degrees for 15 minutes or until brown and bubbly. (You may wish to put grated cheese on top of oysters before baking, but I do not because my husband doesn't like it.)

Baked Oysters–Casino

2	sticks butter, softened
½	cup chopped parsley
½	cup lemon juice
1	tablespoon chopped lemon zest
2	tablespoons Worcestershire sauce
1	tablespoon capers (optional)
1	ounce sherry
1	ounce brandy
2	anchovy fillets
2	dozen oysters, shucked and on the half shell
6	slices bacon, cut into quarters
	Chef Hans Creole seasoning to taste, or salt and pepper to taste

These make a great appetizer.

Combine butter, parsley, lemon juice, lemon zest, Worcestershire sauce, capers, sherry, brandy and anchovy fillets in a food processor or blender. Chop on high speed until mixture is light and fluffy. Spread mixture evenly over oysters. Top each with a piece of bacon. For added color and taste, sprinkle oysters with Creole seasoning. Place oysters on a baking pan. Bake at 325 degrees for 15 to 20 minutes.

SOFT-SHELL CRAB:

A CREOLE DELICACY

In New Orleans and other cities where great cuisine is king, the soft-shelled crab is considered the ultimate delight in seafood. In order to grow, the blue crab occasionally must shed, or back out, of its rigid shell. In sea-water, the new shell remains soft for a few hours to allow the crab to stretch to a larger size, then hardens again. In this soft state, the crab is a special table delicacy. It can be prepared in a variety of imaginative ways and eaten – shell and all.

Crab Stuffed Tomatoes

5	large firm tomatoes
¾	cup finely chopped onions
½	cup finely chopped bell pepper
4	tablespoons butter or margarine
1	cup Italian breadcrumbs
¼	cup freshly grated Parmesan cheese
1	pound fresh crabmeat
	salt and pepper to taste

Cut off a ⅛-inch thick slice from the top of each tomato. Scoop out and reserve pulp. Sauté onions and bell pepper in butter in a skillet. Add breadcrumbs, cheese and crabmeat. Season with salt and pepper. Add about half of reserved tomato pulp and mix well. Stuff mixture into tomato shells. Place shells in a greased shallow pan. Bake at 350 degrees for 25 minutes.

My son-in-law, Bernard, introduced me to stuffed tomatoes. This is my own version with crabmeat. However, the crabmeat may be omitted or other seafood can be substituted. Very delicious!

Crabmeat Casserole

2	pounds crabmeat
1	cup mayonnaise
2	cups half-and-half or evaporated milk
2	tablespoons flour
	salt and pepper to taste
1	cup finely chopped onion
4	hard-boiled eggs, chopped
1	tablespoon lemon juice
¼	cup finely chopped parsley

Combine all ingredients and mix well. Transfer to a baking dish and allow to stand for 30 minutes. Bake at 350 degrees for 30 minutes.

This is a new dish I prepare when I'm in a hurry (and crabmeat is not too expensive). I just throw it all together, bake and enjoy!

Crabmeat Special

1	cup mayonnaise
¾	cup freshly grated Parmesan cheese
1	cup finely chopped green onions
3	14 ounce cans (or jars) artichoke hearts, drained and thinly sliced
1	pound fresh crabmeat
	juice of 1 lemon
	salt and pepper to taste

Combine all ingredients and pour into a 3-quart casserole dish. Bake at 350 degrees for 30 minutes. Serve hot. Serves 6.

This is such a special dish and so quick and easy to fix. All I fix with this is my frozen fruit salad, a green vegetable and bread. It can also be used as a dip. Funny how I've learned to do new and modern dishes — wish my Mama would be here to enjoy this!

Marinated Crab Fingers

2	tablespoons white or cider vinegar
1	tablespoon oil
	salt and pepper to taste
1	tablespoon chopped green onions
1	teaspoon chopped parsley
1	16 ounce bottle 1000 Island dressing
	dash of Worcestershire sauce (optional)
1	pound crab fingers (fresh are best)

Combine all ingredients except crab. Add crab to mixture and marinate in refrigerator for at least 1 hour.

This is one of my children's favorite. I usually keep this in refrigerator overnight, that is if they last that long.

Crabmeat Dressing

1	medium onion, chopped
¼	medium bell pepper, chopped
5	tablespoons butter or margarine
1	pound crabmeat
5	slices white bread, toasted
¼	cup water
1	egg, beaten
	salt and pepper
	plain breadcrumbs

Sauté onions and bell pepper in butter until onions are translucent. Add crabmeat and sauté. Soak bread in water to dampen. Squeeze out excess water and mash bread into small pieces in a bowl. Mix in egg. Add sautéed mixture and mix well. Season with salt and pepper. Spoon mixture into crab shells. Lightly sprinkle breadcrumbs on top. Bake at 350 degrees for 20 to 25 minutes.

Fried Crab Claws

1	pound crab claws
2	eggs, beaten
2	cups flour
	salt and pepper to taste
	oil for deep frying

Dip crab claws in eggs until coated, then dredge crab in flour seasoned with salt and pepper. Drop crab claws into hot oil and fry until golden brown. Remove from heat and enjoy!

Soft-Shelled Crabs Meunière or Amandine

1	cup milk
1	egg
4	large soft-shelled crabs
	salt and pepper to taste
1½	cups flour
	oil for deep frying
1½	sticks butter
1	tablespoon lemon juice
¼	teaspoon white pepper

In a large bowl, beat together milk and egg until well blended. Season crabs with salt and pepper. Soak crabs in milk mixture for 15 minutes, turning frequently. Dredge crabs in flour and shake off excess. Lower crabs into a pot of 365 degree oil, being careful not to overcrowd the pot. The crabs should have room to float on the surface of the oil. Fry crabs 5 to 6 minutes or until they are golden brown. Transfer crabs to paper towels to drain. Keep crabs warm in a 200 degree oven.

In a heavy saucepan, melt butter over low heat until it begins to brown. Remove from heat and add lemon juice and pepper. Mix well and return to low heat. Cook 1 minute or until meunière sauce is nut brown. Serve the crabs with a generous portion of meunière sauce poured over each serving. Serves 2 to 4.

Amandine: Prepare recipe as above, adding 1 cup blanched sliced almonds to butter just before it browns. Remove almonds as they brown and reserve them in a small bowl until sauce is complete. To serve, spread almonds over crabs and pour sauce on top. Serves 2 to 4.

These are very special recipes! Crabs are my favorite seafood and soft-shelled crabs are the best of the best. I used to eat the sautéed buster crabs at Manchac on my way to New Orleans. They quit sautéing the crabs there but I still enjoy them in my kitchen. Of course, it tastes as good but a lot more preparation on my part — plus cleaning up after.

Soft-Shelled Crab à la Pontchartrain

6	large soft-shelled crabs, cleaned
	salt and pepper to taste
2	eggs
½	cup milk
	flour
4	tablespoons margarine
2	tablespoons olive oil
	parsley sprigs and lemon slices for garnish

Season crabs with salt and pepper including under top shell. Beat together eggs and milk. Roll crabs in flour, dip in egg mixture, then roll in flour again. Melt margarine in a skillet and add olive oil. Pan fry crabs in skillet on both sides until golden brown. Drain crabs on paper towels. Place crabs on a platter and pour cheese sauce on top. Garnish with parsley sprigs and lemon slices.

Cheese Sauce

1	stick margarine
¼	cup cornstarch
2	cups milk
1	cup cubed Velveeta
¼	teaspoon black pepper
1	handful chopped shallots

Melt margarine in a saucepan. Stir in cornstarch. Remove from heat and blend in milk, Velveeta, pepper and shallots. Return to medium heat. Cook, stirring constantly, until sauce comes to a slow boil and starts to thicken. Remove from heat.

Delete cheese and add sautéed shrimp or crawfish tails.

Soft-Shelled Crabs à la Creole

12   **soft shelled crabs, cleaned**
      salt and pepper to taste
2   **cups buttermilk**
4   **teaspoons sifted flour**
      butter, melted
      parsley sprigs and lemon wedges for garnish

Season crabs with salt and pepper. Season buttermilk with salt and pepper. Soak crabs in milk until crabs are thoroughly saturated with milk. Remove crabs from milk and pat lightly with flour. Brush crabs with melted butter and broil slowly for 15 minutes or until delicately browned and cooked thoroughly. Serve on a platter garnished with parsley sprigs and lemon wedges. Drizzle a small amount of melted butter over crabs and sprinkle with chopped parsley.

FISH

This was Lucy Suzanne's first *big* catch. She had a great time catching these with her Aunt Missey. Then we all enjoyed eating them but only after two went to the taxidermist for mounting!

I had only eaten stuffed flounder once at our camp – Daddy never went deep sea fishing to be able to bring any home for Mama to cook. Teddy Duhon served this then and I'll never forget how good it was! Several years later, Harry went deep sea fishing and brought home some beautiful flounder for me to cook. Not knowing how, I could only try to duplicate Teddy's recipe. And it turned out pretty good – good enough to pass on to you!

Stuffed Flounder

1	cup finely chopped onion
½	cup finely chopped celery
1	teaspoon minced garlic
2	sticks butter or margarine
2	pounds lump crabmeat
2	pounds shrimp, peeled and chopped
2	hamburger buns, crumbled
2	eggs
½	cup chopped green onions
	salt and pepper to taste
5	medium-size flounder, dressed

Sauté onions, celery and garlic in butter until well cooked. Add crabmeat and shrimp. Cook about 10 minutes, stirring often. Cool slightly. Add buns, eggs and green onions. Season to taste with salt and pepper and mix well. Split each flounder in center to make pockets on each side. Stuff seafood mixture into flounder. Broil 12 minutes on each side.

Baked Red Snapper or Red Fish

½ cup oil
½ cup flour
¾ cup chopped onions
¾ cup chopped bell pepper
4 cloves garlic, chopped
1 10 ounce can mild Rotel tomatoes
1 10¾ ounce can condensed tomato soup
½ cup water or as needed
   salt and pepper to taste
1 large red fish or red snapper, dressed
1 cup white wine
   chopped parsley for garnish
   lemon slices for garnish

Make a dark brown roux by combining oil and flour in a saucepan. Cook, stirring constantly, over medium heat. Add onions, bell pepper, garlic, tomatoes and soup. Cook over medium heat for about 1 hour, adding water as needed to make a medium-thick gravy. Season with salt and pepper. Place fish in a roasting pan. Pour tomato gravy and wine over fish. Bake, uncovered, at 350 degrees, basting frequently, for 45 minutes or until fish is done. Carefully lay on a platter. Sprinkle fish with parsley and arrange lemon slices around fish. Serve tomato gravy over rice.

Classic
CAJUN
D E U X

This is a fabulous dish! I is similar to the way Mrs Viyan Simon taught me t bake fish except sh added tomato paste t hers. Not a bad idea bu this is a variation. I enjo both ways. The tomat soup instead of past gives this dish a smootl taste. I enjoy the fishin trips but when I don't ge a chance to go out in th Gulf, there is alway the local Albertson's o Brookshire's where I cal pick up some fish to cool up this tasty dish!

Stuffed Red Snapper

1	medium onion, chopped
½	chopped bell pepper
¼	cup chopped celery
4	tablespoons butter or margarine
1	cup peeled shrimp
1	cup crabmeat
¾	cup breadcrumbs
½	cup chopped green onion tops
	salt and pepper to taste
4-6	pounds red snapper, dressed
4	tablespoons butter, melted
¼	cup lemon juice

Sauté onions, bell pepper and celery in 4 tablespoons butter. Add shrimp, crabmeat, breadcrumbs and green onions. Season with salt and pepper and mix well. Stuff mixture into cavity of fish and place in a pan. Mix 4 tablespoons melted butter with lemon juice and pour over fish in pan. Bake at 350 degrees for 10 minutes per pound of fish, basting often with lemon butter sauce. Serves 6 to 8.

Grilled Salmon

3	large salmon steaks
	salt and pepper to taste
1	teaspoon olive oil
1	teaspoon raspberry vinegar
2	cloves garlic, minced
¼	cup chopped fresh dill
	juice of 1 large lemon

Season salmon with salt and pepper. Combine olive oil, vinegar, garlic, dill and lemon juice and pour over salmon. Marinate salmon about 1 hour.

Heat coals in a bar-b-que pit until hot. Drain salmon, discarding marinade. Place salmon on grill, skin-side down, and cook 5 minutes. Flip over and cook 5 minutes longer. Remove from grill and spread sauce (recipe below) over steaks. Eat while hot. Serves 3.

I never could eat salmon (just wasn't what Cajuns had access to) until my son-in-law served it to me. He really knows how to cook this dish to perfection and he taught me. So now I try to fix it as often as I can purchase the fresh salmon. It's not as good as his so I let him prepare for me as often as I can. I even bought a grilling basket to use, which makes it easier to handle.

Sauce for Salmon

1	stick butter, melted
3	tablespoons ketchup
1	tablespoon Worcestershire sauce
2	tablespoons dry mustard
1	clove garlic, chopped
	pinch of brown sugar
1-2	tablespoons orange juice or orange marmalade

Combine all sauce ingredients.

This sauce is an original by my good friend, Gail. It really adds to the enjoyment of the salmon.

This was not a rare dish in Cajun homes. I'll never forget the first time I went fishing with Mrs. Viyan Simon. I caught a huge garfish. It almost pulled me into the canal! Mrs. Simon had to help me to bring it on ground. Then she cleaned it and cooked it on a fire she made along the levee. She had dug a hole in the ground, made a fire, then set her pot right on top of the fire and fried the garfish. I will never forget that day!

Garfish Patties

3	pounds garfish
3	pounds Irish or red potatoes
1	cup chopped onions
½	cup chopped parsley
4	cloves garlic, finely chopped
5	cups flour, divided
	salt and pepper to taste
¼	cup oil

Grind fish, potatoes, onions, parsley and garlic through an old meat grinder into a large bowl. Add ½ cup flour and mix well. Season with salt and pepper. Form mixture into patties. Season remaining flour with salt and pepper. Dredge patties in flour. Fry in hot oil until brown.

Salmon Croquettes (non Cajun)

1	15½ ounce can pink salmon
	milk
4	tablespoons butter or margarine
¼	cup finely chopped onions
¼	cup flour
½	teaspoon salt
¼	teaspoon black pepper
2	tablespoons chopped green onions
1	tablespoon lemon juice
1	cup dry breadcrumbs, divided
	vegetable oil for frying

Drain salmon, reserving liquid. Add enough milk to reserved liquid to equal 1 cup. Set aside.

Melt butter in a skillet. Add onions and sauté. Stir in flour until smooth. Cook 1 minute, stirring constantly.

(continued on next page)

Salmon Croquettes (non Cajun)....*continued*

Add milk mixture. Cook over low heat, stirring constantly, until sauce is thickened and bubbly. Add salt and pepper; set aside.

Remove skin and bones from salmon and flake with a fork. Add green onions, lemon juice and ½ cup breadcrumbs. Mix in white sauce, stirring well. Refrigerate until thoroughly chilled. Shape mixture into croquettes. (You may wish to make small croquettes as for individuals.) Roll in remaining ½ cup breadcrumbs. Fry croquettes in 3 inches of 375 degree oil until golden brown, or line a pan with foil, spray with Pam, and place croquettes on pan. Bake at 350 to 375 degrees for about 20 to 30 minutes or until golden brown. Delicious! Serves 4.

I made many of these while in high school. Seems like every time we served lunch, Miss Lula Lee Smith, my teacher, made me fix these. They are good!

Sauce
*This is my own personal preference
for a sauce over the croquettes:*

½	**cup peeled and chopped cucumbers**
½	**cup mayonnaise**
½	**cup sour cream**
¼	**cup chopped green onion tops**
½	**teaspoon chopped parsley**
¼	**teaspoon salt**
⅛	**teaspoon black pepper**
1	**can Petit Pois (very small peas), drained**

Put cucumbers, mayonnaise and sour cream in a blender and blend well. Add onion tops, parsley, salt, pepper and peas. Chill. Pour sauce over croquettes and serve.

BREAD

Making bread together really brings out the love Lucy Suzanne and I share. Once this bread is baked, we then share the bread right out of the oven, but only after it is covered with butter and blackberry jelly!

I had not heard of this type of cornbread until recently. This is a very typical dish in South Louisiana now. When I was a girl, the typical cornbread was served with syrup and milk (one of my daddy's favorites). I wouldn't recommend doing that to this recipe.

I recently went on a trip along the East Coast with my friends, Beverly and Harold. While touring, I enjoyed my first pop-over. So I immediately purchased a popover pan and started baking this wonderful hot bread. I bet I could even add a choco-late pudding inside and have a great dessert as well as a bread.

Shrimp or Crawfish Cornbread

2	eggs, beaten
1	16 ounce can cream style corn
¼	cup oil
¼	cup grated Cheddar cheese
1	cup yellow cornmeal
½	teaspoon baking soda
1	teaspoon salt
1	cup raw shrimp, peeled, deveined and coarsely chopped, or crawfish
2	tablespoons grated onion
1	small jalapeño pepper (optional)

Combine eggs, corn, oil and cheese. Mix well. Stir in cornmeal, baking soda, salt, shrimp, onion and jalapeño pepper. Mix and pour into a greased or sprayed with PAM hot 9x13 inch pan. Bake at 350 degrees for 45 minutes.

Popovers

3	eggs
1½	cups all-purpose flour
1½	cups milk
½	teaspoon salt
1	tablespoon unsalted butter, melted

Beat eggs slightly in a mixing bowl. Add remaining in-gredients and beat until smooth; do not overbeat. Pour batter into the cups of a popover pan that has been sprayed with PAM, filling each three-fourths full. Bake at 450 degrees for 15 minutes. Reduce heat to 325 degrees and bake 25 to 30 minutes longer or until golden brown. Serve immediately. Makes 6 popovers.

Never Fail Ice Box Rolls

2　cups sweet milk, or 1 cup water and 1 cup milk
½　cup sugar
½　cup shortening
1　teaspoon salt
2　packages active dry yeast
6　cups sifted flour
　　melted butter

Pour milk into a saucepan. Add sugar and shortening and heat to scald milk but do not boil. Remove from heat and add salt. Cool to lukewarm. Add yeast and stir until dissolved. Gradually beat in flour. Toss dough onto a board and knead lightly. Place dough back into pan. Let dough rise 1½ to 2 hours. Remove dough from pan and knead down. Pinch off small amounts of dough and roll out to ½ inch thick. Cut dough with a biscuit cutter. Dip rolls in melted butter and fold over. Place rolls in pan and cover. Let rise 1½ to 2 hours longer. Bake at 350 degrees for about 15 minutes. Refrigerate remaining dough and let rise as above when making into rolls. Dough will keep, well covered, for 5 to 6 days.

These are the best rolls I have ever made. The recipe comes from an old friend of mine of years ago, Mrs. M. D. Hughes. These will never fail, and are delicious!

Ollie's Biscuits

4　cups Pioneer buttermilk biscuit mix
1　cup sour cream
1　cup diet 7-Up
　　pinch of baking powder
2　tablespoons sugar
1　stick butter, melted

Combine all ingredients except melted butter. Roll out dough and cut with a biscuit cutter. Place biscuits on a baking sheet and drizzle with melted butter. Bake at 375 degrees for 20 to 25 minutes.

I could never bake a good biscuit. So my sister-in-law, Ollie Marie, gave me this recipe to use. I now make delicious biscuits and if I can, anyone can.

This recipe can be cut down, dividing by 2 or 3 to produce how many you want. I usually make the whole recipe because I freeze the biscuits and bake as I need them. (I eat at least one a day.) To freeze, I place the unbaked biscuits on a baking sheet and freeze until solid. Then I take them, put them in a zip-loc bag and keep them in the freezer. To bake, simply pop into a preheated 300 degree oven for 20 minutes, then increase to 350 degrees for 5 more minutes. They are delicious with my blackberry jelly!

Cheddar Cheese Biscuits

3	cups flour
1½	teaspoons baking powder
2	tablespoons sugar
2	teaspoons salt
2½	cups heavy whipping cream
1	cup grated Cheddar cheese
3	tablespoons butter, melted

Combine flour, baking powder, sugar and salt in a large bowl. Add cream and cheese and stir gently, mixing just until dough holds together. Turn dough onto a lightly floured board and knead over twice; do not over handle dough. Roll out dough to about 1-inch thick and cut with a biscuit cutter or a drinking glass. Place on a baking sheet and let stand for 10 minutes to produce a taller, lighter biscuit. Brush top of biscuits lightly with melted butter. Bake at 375 degrees for about 20 minutes. Makes about 35 to 40 biscuits.

Cinnamon Rolls

Dough

1	package active dry yeast
½	cup sugar, divided
1½	cups warm water, divided
1	teaspoon salt
¼	cup shortening
1	egg
5	cups flour (approximately)

Filling

1	cup sugar
3	tablespoons cinnamon
1	stick butter, melted

I used to make cinnamon rolls for my children. I didn't mind the mess because I enjoyed them also. There sure were no canned cinnamon rolls in those days! But I think mine were Grand!

Combine yeast, 2 tablespoons sugar and ½ cup warm water in a small bowl. Let stand about 10 minutes. In a large bowl, combine salt, shortening, egg and remaining sugar and remaining water. Mix well. Add yeast mixture. Stir in enough flour to make a kneadable dough. Knead for about 10 minutes. Let dough rise in a warm place until it has doubled in bulk. Working with a small amount of dough at a time, turn dough onto a floured board and roll to about ¼-inch thick.

To prepare filling, mix sugar and cinnamon. Spread melted butter over rolled out dough. Sprinkle cinnamon sugar mixture on top. Roll dough like a jelly roll and cut crosswise into ½-inch thick rounds. Place rolls in a baking pan sprayed with PAM and let rise for about 30 to 40 minutes. Bake at 375 degrees for 35 minutes. Remove from pan immediately after baking.

My neighbor, Gloria Abraugh, served these rolls one night when we went for supper. They were the best I have ever eaten. The electricity went out but we ate by candle-light — did not ruin our supper at all. I even learned to eat and enjoy rare beef.

Butter Rolls

¾   cup milk
¼   cup sugar
1   teaspoon salt
4   tablespoons margarine
½   cup warm water (105 to 115 degrees)
2   packages active dry yeast
1   egg
3½   cups unsifted flour, divided

Scald milk. Stir in sugar, salt and margarine. Cool to luke-warm. Pour warm water into a large, warm bowl. Sprinkle yeast over water and stir until dissolved. Add lukewarm milk mixture, egg and 2 cups flour. Beat until smooth. Stir in enough of remaining flour to make a soft dough. Cover and let rise in a warm, draft-free place for 30 minutes or until doubled in bulk. Punch down dough and shape into 24 rolls. Place rolls on a greased baking sheet, or in cake pans or muffin cups. Cover and let rise in a warm place for 30 minutes or until doubled in bulk. Bake at 400 degrees for 15 minutes. Makes 2 dozen rolls.

Bread Pudding
mix 2 cup sugar with 8 egg yolks. Break up 18 slices of Bread, and add to creamed mixture. add 7½ cups milk, Evaporated and reg. milk. 2 tsp Vanila, 1 Cup melted margarine or butter. Bake at 400° till knife comes out Clean. Make meringue with egg white — ½ tsp cream of tartar and 12 TBS. Sugar Spread on top of cooked Pudding and Brown.

Mama used this recipe often. It made a big dish for a crowd of hungry eaters. This was also Daddy's choice of dessert, along with her Ginger Bread.

Refrigerated Butter Rolls

1¾   **cups milk**

¾   **cup shortening**

½   **cup sugar**

1   **teaspoon salt**

½   **cup warm water (105 to 115 degrees)**

2   **packages active dry yeast**

2   **eggs**

5   **cups flour**

    melted butter

Gloria also shared another recipe for rolls which I enjoy making. Can't make up my mind which one I prefer.

Scald milk. Stir in shortening, sugar and salt. Cool to lukewarm. Pour warm water into a large, warm bowl. Sprinkle yeast over water and stir until dissolved. Add lukewarm milk mixture, eggs and 2 cups flour. Beat with an electric mixer until smooth. Stir in remaining flour to make a soft dough. Cover and let rise in a warm, draft-free place until doubled in bulk. Turn dough out onto a floured cloth and knead. Place dough in a greased bowl, cover and refrigerate until ready to use. Punch down and roll out dough on a floured cloth. Use a cutter to cut out rolls. Spread melted butter on rolls, fold over and top with more butter. Place on a baking sheet and let rise. Bake at 375 degrees for about 20 minutes.

Old Time Doughnuts

3	cups sugar
1	tablespoon nutmeg
7	teaspoons baking powder
4	eggs
¼	cup oil
2	cups milk
7	cups flour or as needed
	oil for deep frying
	powdered sugar for sprinkling

Mix sugar, nutmeg and baking powder. Mix in eggs and oil. Add milk and mix well. Stir in flour, using more if dough is too soft. Roll out dough and cut with a doughnut cutter. Fry doughnuts in hot oil until golden brown. Sprinkle with powdered sugar.

Gingerbread

1	cup sugar
2	sticks butter or shortening, softened
4	eggs, well beaten
2	cups cane syrup
2	teaspoons baking soda
2	cups boiling water or buttermilk
5	cups flour
1	teaspoon cinnamon
1	teaspoon ground cloves
1	teaspoon ground ginger

Cream sugar and butter. Add eggs and beat well. Mix in cane syrup. Dissolve baking soda in boiling water and add to creamed mixture. Mix well. Combine flour, cinnamon, cloves and ginger in a separate bowl. Add dry ingredients, one cup at a time, to creamed mixture. Beat well and pour into a baking pan sprayed with PAM. Bake at 350 degrees for 40 minutes or until done. Serve hot or cold.

Ginger Bread   350°

1 C. Sugar   1. Beat Sugar and shortening
2 C. Molasses   2. Add Syrup, soda and Hot water
1 C. Shortening   3. Sift flour and spices at to
1 tsp cinn   mixture.
1 tsp cloves   4. Add well beaten eggs last.
1 tsp ginger   5. Bake in 350° oven about
2 tsp b. soda dissolve in   40 min or until pick
2 cups boiling water   comes out clean. Serve
5 C. flour   Hot with whipped cream
4 C. Well beaten eggs   2 TSP Barking Powder

This card is a treasure for me! It really excited me more to find it.

Classic
CAJUN
D E U X

SALADS

Seems like I found
the perfect tomato
for my salad. All I
need now is salt and
pepper! Nothing like
vine ripe tomatoes
for a Cajun salad.

Simple But Delicious Ambrosia

6	oranges, peeled and sliced
½	cup powdered sugar
1	cup coconut

Mix all ingredients together. Refrigerate before serving.

5-Cup Salad

1	cup coconut
1	cup Mandarin oranges, drained
1	cup crushed pineapple, drained
1	cup sour cream
1	cup mini marshmallows

Combine all ingredients and stir well. Cover and refrigerate until ready to serve. Serves 6.

Cajun Waldorf Salad

3	Granny Smith apples, chopped
2	stalks celery, finely chopped
½	cup mayonnaise
1	teaspoon Dijon mustard
1	cup fresh pineapple chunks
1	cup roasted pecans

Mix together all ingredients well. Chill before serving.

Fruit Salad with Fruit Salad Dressing

3	Golden Delicious apples, chopped or diced
2	oranges, peeled and chopped
3	bananas, sliced
1	16 ounce can fruit cocktail, undrained
1	16 ounce can peaches, undrained and chopped
1	16 ounce can pears, undrained and chopped
1	10 ounce jar maraschino cherries, undrained
½	cup sugar or 2 packages Nutrasweet

Mix all ingredients together. Refrigerate for several hours or overnight before serving. Serves 6 to 8.

This was my mother-in-law's favorite dish at holidays — she always fixed this herself being she did not like to cook. But this was her specialty as she allowed no one else to prepare the fruit salad. Now, whenever I go for a visit, I make it for her to enjoy. (Just doesn't seem to taste as good as her's did, however.)

Mama's Potato Salad

6	large potatoes, boiled, peeled and chopped
¼	cup finely chopped celery
¼	cup finely chopped onions
6	hard-boiled eggs, peeled and chopped
	salt and pepper to taste
1	cup mayonnaise
1	tablespoon prepared yellow mustard

Place potatoes in a large bowl. Add celery, onions and eggs. Use a potato masher or fork to mash together all ingredients. Season with salt and pepper. Add mayonnaise and mustard. Mix well. Serves 6.

This was my mother's favorite potato salad — and she made a lot of it many times. Potato salad was always the salad of our choice, and it still is today. Never had gumbo without it!

Classic CAJUN DEUX

Cajuns do not serve many salads with their meals — guess it's because we save our appetites for the main course. But this is one salad that is enjoyed by all and isn't too filling!

Old Fashioned Wilted Salad

2   tablespoons salad oil

4   teaspoons cider vinegar

2   teaspoons sugar

4   cups shredded leaf lettuce

1   cup chopped green onions

2   slices bacon, fried crisp and crumbled

2   hard-boiled eggs, peeled and sliced

Heat oil, vinegar and sugar until very hot. Combine lettuce and green onions in a bowl. Pour heated mixture over lettuce and onions and toss lightly. Top with bacon and sliced eggs. Serves 4.

When I was working in Farm Bureau, we had several dinners. One of the favorite dishes was the layered salad. Rhonda Bostick always brought it to serve. Everyone really enjoyed it.

Layered Salad

1   head lettuce

1   large onion, sliced

1   cup sliced mushrooms

1   10 ounce can green peas, drained

1   cup mayonnaise

1   cup freshly grated Parmesan cheese

8   ounces bacon, fried crisp and crumbled

3   hard-boiled eggs, sliced

1   large tomato, diced

Layer lettuce, onions, mushrooms, peas, mayonnaise and cheese. Refrigerate. When ready to serve, top with layers of bacon, eggs and tomatoes.

Potato, White Bean and Corn Salad

2	pounds red potatoes, cooked, peeled and cubed
1	15 ounce jar cooked white beans or lima beans, drained
1	15 ounce can corn, drained
2	cups green onions, chopped fine, 2 tablespoons reserved for garnish
2	medium bell peppers, chopped fine
⅓	cup olive oil
1½	tablespoons lemon juice
¼	cup mayonnaise
½	tablespoon sugar
	salt and pepper to taste
	lemon pepper to taste
¼	cup creamy Italian dressing
¼	cup Ranch dressing
1	cup shredded cheese of choice

Combine potatoes, beans, corn, green onions and bell pepper in a bowl and toss. In a separate large bowl, whisk together oil, lemon juice, mayonnaise, sugar, salt, pepper and lemon pepper. Fold in vegetable mixture and dressings, adding more dressing if needed to coat vegetables. Sprinkle reserved green onions and cheese on top. Refrigerate 1 hour before serving.

I have a huge collection
cookbooks which I u:
This is one of the ma
recipes I use after
revised it. It is differe
on my Cajun table setti
but so easy to make f
a crowd.

Salad Dressings

We did not use many salad dressings when I was growing up. Mama never made any, but I have learned to make and appreciate them. These dressings came from my Home Ec. class many years ago.

Basic Mayonnaise

2	egg yolks or whole eggs
1	teaspoon salt
1	teaspoon dry mustard
1	teaspoon sugar
2	tablespoons vinegar
2	cups salad oil
3	tablespoons lemon juice
1	tablespoon hot water

Place egg yolks in a small mixing bowl. Add salt, mustard and sugar and blend. Add vinegar and mix well. Add oil, 1 teaspoon at a time, using a mixer on low speed, until ¼ cup oil has been added. Increase mixer to high and slowly add remaining oil, alternating last ½ cup with lemon juice. Add hot water and beat well to remove oily appearance.

Hot Bacon-Vinegar Dressing

2	strips raw bacon, minced
½	cup water
¼	cup vinegar
1	tablespoon sugar
½	teaspoon salt
¼	teaspoon black pepper

Cook bacon in a skillet over medium heat until crisp. Add all remaining ingredients to skillet and bring to a boil. Serve immediately over leaf lettuce or shredded spinach. Makes ¾ cup.

Vinaigrette Dressing

2	tablespoons finely chopped sour pickles
2	tablespoons finely chopped green bell pepper
2	tablespoons finely chopped parsley
1½	teaspoons salt
⅛	teaspoon black pepper
⅛	teaspoon cayenne pepper
1	hard-boiled egg, chopped
⅛	teaspoon paprika
1	clove garlic, grated (optional)
½	cup olive oil
2	tablespoons cider vinegar

Combine all ingredients in a jar and shake well. Chill several hours before serving.

Basic French Dressing

1½	cups salad oil
½	cup vinegar
2	teaspoons salt
2	tablespoons lemon juice
1	teaspoon sugar
½	teaspoon black pepper
½	teaspoon dry mustard

Mix together all ingredients in a blender or place in a quart jar and shake vigorously.

Caesar Salad Dressing: To ½ cup French Dressing, add ¼ teaspoon dry mustard and 1 beaten raw egg. Serve on tossed greens with crunchy bits of toasted crusty bread.

Tomato French Dressing

1	10¾ ounce can condensed tomato soup
1	onion, grated
¼	cup sugar
1	tablespoon salt
1	teaspoon prepared mustard
1	cup vinegar
1	clove garlic
1	tablespoon Worcestershire sauce
1	cup salad oil

Mix together all ingredients in a blender or place in a quart jar and shake vigorously. Store in refrigerator.

Fruit Salad Dressing

½	cup syrup from canned peaches
1	tablespoon sugar or to taste
2	egg yolks, well beaten
⅛	teaspoon salt
⅛	teaspoon paprika
1½	teaspoons lemon juice

Heat peach syrup in a saucepan over medium heat. Combine sugar, egg yolks, salt and paprika in a bowl. Slowly add peach syrup, stirring constantly. Return to saucepan and cook over low heat until thick and smooth. Remove from heat and slowly add lemon juice. Mix thoroughly and chill. Sweeten with extra sugar as desired. Serve with all fruit salads. Other fruit juices may be substituted for the peach syrup.

Poppy Seed Dressing

⅓   **cup honey**
½   **teaspoon salt**
⅓   **cup vinegar**
3   **tablespoons prepared mustard (optional)**
2½   **tablespoons poppy seeds**
1¼   **cups salad oil**
1   **tablespoon grated onion (optional)**

Combine all ingredients in order listed in a small mixing bowl or blender. Beat until oil is blended and mixture is thick and creamy. Pour dressing into a jar and chill. Store in refrigerator. Excellent on fruit salads, especially citrus and avocado.

Special Salad Dressing

1   **0.75 ounce package dry garlic and herb salad dressing mix**
¼   **cup extra virgin olive oil**
⅓   **cup balsamic vinegar**
⅛   **teaspoon salt**
⅛   **teaspoon black pepper**
½   **tablespoon dry Ranch buttermilk salad dressing mix**

Combine all ingredients and mix well.

Beverly McCormack taught my daughter how to make this salad dressing. Melissa has served this several times over a green garden salad. She enjoys it as much as the guests.

VEGETABLES

Nothing is more fun
than Lucy Suzanne
and me cooking
together! She really
loves vegetables
and is always ready
to show me how they
are cooked.

Spinach Florentine

1	medium onion, chopped
2	tablespoons butter
1	10 ounce package frozen chopped spinach, thawed, rinsed and drained
	salt and pepper to taste
¼	cup sour cream

Sauté onions in butter. Add spinach and cook 20 minutes over medium heat. Season with salt and pepper. Stir in sour cream and heat. Serve hot.

Stuffed Mirlitons

4	whole mirlitons
1	medium onion, chopped
1	clove garlic, minced
8	ounces shrimp, ham or ground beef
3	tablespoons butter or margarine
1	cup breadcrumbs
	salt and pepper to taste
1	egg, beaten
¼	cup chopped green onions

Boil mirlitons in water for 45 minutes or until tender. Cut each mirliton in half and remove seeds. Scoop out pulp with a spoon, leaving a ⅛-inch thick shell and reserving pulp. Sauté onions, garlic and shrimp in butter for 10 minutes or until shrimp are cooked. Add reserved mirliton pulp, breadcrumbs and salt and pepper. Cook about 5 minutes longer, stirring well. Cool slightly and add egg and green onions. Stuff mixture into mirliton shells. Bake at 350 degrees for 30 minutes. Serves 8.

Butter Beans (Limas)

2   medium onions, chopped
1   clove garlic, chopped
½   cup bacon drippings
1   ham bone, or 4 ounces ham
2½   pounds fresh or dried butter beans
2½   quarts water
      salt and pepper to taste

Sauté onions and garlic in bacon drippings until onions are transparent. Add ham bone, beans and water. Season with salt and pepper. Bring to a boil. Reduce heat and simmer until beans are tender - about 45 minutes for fresh beans or 1½ hours for dried. You may need to add more water if beans start to stick or become dry.

My father did not like vegetables but Mama cooked butter beans often. She and I really enjoyed this with our rice and gravy. Canned or frozen butter beans can be used.

Eggplant Casserole

1   medium eggplant, chopped
3   tablespoons bacon drippings
½   cup diced onions
2   tablespoons margarine
1   14.5 ounce can tomatoes, chopped
1   tablespoon chopped parsley
1   teaspoon sugar
      salt and pepper to taste
1   cup buttered breadcrumbs
½   cup coarsely shredded cheese

Sauté eggplant in bacon drippings for 5 to 6 minutes. Transfer to a baking dish. Sauté onions in margarine until yellow. Add tomatoes, parsley, sugar and salt and pepper. Stir and bring to a boil. Pour mixture over eggplant. Sprinkle with breadcrumbs and cheese. Bake at 350 degrees for 45 minutes.

I am always looking for new ways to fix vegetables. As I was searching through my childhood recipe files, I ran across this recipe. It isn't new, but I am enjoying it because I had actually forgotten about it.

I had never made these until my sister-in-law, Susie, gave me her recipe. What a pleasant surprise! Very tasty! They are better than hush-puppies as far as I'm concerned! And can be served at any meal.

Eggplant Balls

1	eggplant, peeled and chopped
½	teaspoon baking powder
½	teaspoon sugar
½	cup chopped green onions
½	cup flour
½	teaspoon salt
1	egg
	pepper to taste
	oil for deep frying

Cook eggplant in boiling water. Drain and mash. Add all remaining ingredients except oil and mix well. Drop batter by spoonfuls into hot oil. Cook until golden brown. These look like hushpuppies.

Mama had never made potato cakes, probably mainly because we never had leftover mashed potatoes. My mother-in-law is the one who introduced me to them. It's a great way to make use of leftover mashed potatoes. The cakes can be served for breakfast or with your regular meal!

Mashed Potato Cakes

2	cups mashed potatoes
1	egg, beaten
2	tablespoons flour
¼	cup chopped green onions
	salt and pepper to taste
	oil to cover bottom of skillet

Mix together potatoes and egg. Stir in flour and green onions. Season with salt and pepper. Shape mixture into ½-inch thick patties. Heat oil in a skillet. Brown patties on both sides in oil. Enjoy at any meal.

Carrot Soufflé

2　pounds carrots, sliced
4　eggs, separated
1　stick butter or margarine, softened
2　heaping teaspoons flour
2　heaping teaspoons baking powder
1　cup sugar
1　tablespoon vanilla
　　powdered sugar

Boil carrots in water until softened. Drain and place carrots in a food processor. Add egg yolks, butter, flour, baking powder, sugar and vanilla. Blend until well mixed. Beat egg whites until stiff and fold into mixture. Pour mixture into a 2-quart glass baking dish. Bake at 350 degrees for 45 minutes. Remove from oven and sprinkle with powdered sugar. Serve warm.

Tater Tot Casserole

1　cup chopped onions
1　cup chopped bell pepper
1　cup chopped celery
1　pound smoked sausage, sliced
1　stick margarine
1　10½ ounce can condensed cream of chicken soup
1　10¾ ounce can condensed cream of mushroom soup
1　cup shredded cheese
　　salt and pepper to taste
1　16 ounce package frozen tater tots

Sauté onions, bell pepper, celery and sausage in margarine in a skillet. Drain grease and add soups and cheese to skillet. Cook until cheese is melted and smooth. Season with salt and pepper. Layer half of tater tots and half of soup mixture in a baking pan. Repeat layers. Bake at 350 degrees for 1 hour.

This is something new I ate at Piccadilly. It is almost like sweet potato casserole. I really don't like carrots, but this is so different and delicious! And great for those who don't like carrots (you cannot taste the carrots.)

Susie, my sister-in-law, gave me this recipe to try. It really makes a great casserole to bring to family functions or socials and goes with mostly any other dish.

Onion Cheese Casserole

5-6	onions, sliced ¼-inch thick
1	stick butter
	bread slices
1	10¾ ounce can cream of mushroom soup
1	tablespoon salt
1	tablespoon black pepper
1	teaspoon celery salt
8	ounces sharp Cheddar cheese, shredded

Sauté onions in butter until softened. Cover the bottom of a 2-quart casserole dish with bread slices. Scatter sautéed onions on top. Spread half of soup over onions and season with salt, pepper and celery salt. Spread with remaining half of soup. Top with cheese. Bake at 325 degrees for 25 to 30 minutes. Casserole can be covered with plastic wrap before baking and refrigerated for up to 1 day until ready to bake. Serves 5 to 6.

Stove Top BBQ Beans

4	slices bacon, cut into ¼-inch pieces
¼	cup chopped onions
¼	cup chopped bell pepper
1	15 ounce can pork and beans
½	cup BBQ sauce
½	cup ketchup
3	tablespoons prepared mustard
¼	cup brown sugar
	salt and pepper to taste

Brown bacon pieces in a pot. Add onions and bell pepper and sauté until starting to soften. Add beans, BBQ sauce, ketchup, mustard, brown sugar and salt and pepper. Cook over medium heat for 20 minutes, stirring often to prevent sticking.

Tomato Aspic

1	10¾ ounce can condensed tomato soup
2	cups V-8 juice or tomato juice
1	8 ounce package cream cheese
3	envelopes unflavored gelatin
½	cup cold water
	salt and pepper to taste
¾	cup mayonnaise
¾	cup finely chopped bell pepper
½	cup finely chopped celery
¼	cup finely chopped green onion tops
1	medium avocado, finely chopped
¾	cup finely chopped onion

Heat soup and juice in a saucepan. Add cream cheese and stir until blended well. Dissolve gelatin in cold water and add to soup mixture. Season with salt and pepper. Stir in mayonnaise, bell pepper, celery, onion tops, avocado and onions. Pour mixture into a large mold or 12 individual molds. Chill until set. Serves 12.

My son-in-law's mother, Sue McKenzie, makes the best aspic I have ever eaten. She told me she had already added boiled or sautéed chopped shrimp to it also. But I prefer the plain one. This is so delightful and a dish to be proud to serve at any social, or simply just for your family.

Dip for Raw Vegetables

1	8 ounce container sour cream
1	cup mayonnaise
1½	teaspoons grated onion
½	teaspoon Worcestershire sauce
1	teaspoon dry mustard
	chopped green onion tops to taste
1	teaspoon horseradish
1	clove garlic, chopped fine
¼-½	teaspoon lemon pepper

Combine all ingredients. Chill several hours or overnight. Serve with raw vegetables. Makes 2 cups.

This is very popular at all the weddings and socials. I don't enjoy raw vegetables, but the dip is delicious on a cracker!

Creamed Spinach

1	bunch spinach or two 10 ounce packages frozen
2	cups water
3	tablespoons margarine or butter
1	tablespoon finely chopped onion
1	clove garlic, finely chopped
1	tablespoon flour
½	cup hot cream or half-and-half
1	teaspoon sugar
	salt and pepper to taste
⅛	teaspoon nutmeg
	zest of ½ lemon
1	hard-boiled egg, sliced

Pick over and cut roots and tough stems from spinach. Bring water to a rapid boil. Add spinach, reduce heat and simmer about 10 to 15 minutes. Drain and chop fine or purée. Melt margarine in a skillet. Add onions and garlic and cook until golden brown. Stir in flour until blended. Stir in hot cream and sugar and cook until smooth. Add spinach and cook 3 to 4 minutes. Season with salt, pepper, nutmeg and lemon zest. Garnish with egg slices.

Fried Green Tomatoes

1	cup cornmeal
	salt and pepper to taste
2	large green tomatoes, sliced ⅛-inch thick
	oil for deep frying

Season cornmeal with salt and pepper in a bowl. Coat tomatoes on both sides with seasoned cornmeal. Heat oil in a large heavy skillet. Drop tomato slices into hot oil and fry 3 to 5 minutes on both sides or until golden brown. Remove slices immediately and drain. Serve hot. Serves 3.

Smothered Okra

1	large onion, chopped
¼	cup oil
1	medium tomato, peeled and chopped
2	pounds fresh okra, sliced ¼-inch thick
	salt and pepper to taste

Sauté onions in oil for about 2 minutes. Add tomato and okra and cook over medium heat for about 45 minutes. Season with salt and pepper. Serves 6.

Mama cooked this and I always enjoyed it. I passed it on to my daughter, Melissa — I think she cooks it even better than I do. It's so simple to cook, yet so good! If you don't have a tomato, you can use canned tomatoes; also frozen okra can be used.

Okra and Tomatoes à Bernard

¾	cup water
1	tablespoon vinegar
1	small onion, sliced
2	tablespoons sugar
1	pound okra, cut into ½-inch pieces
2	small tomatoes, chopped
	salt and pepper to taste

Bring a saucepan with water, vinegar, onions and sugar to a boil. Add okra and cook until tender. Add tomatoes and season with salt and pepper. Cook until tomatoes are tender and water is almost all evaporated. Serve hot.

My son-in-law, Bernard, is a pretty good cook. He has learned from me as I have learned from him. This is something he just throws together — pretty good!

This is an old time favorite of my family. We always had a jar of Cornichon in our refrigerator, and I still do, especially when my son-in-law, Bernard, or my friends, Lonnie and Freddie, enjoy a meal with us. As I use up all the hot pickled cucumbers, I simply add more to the same jar of peppers. These peppers usually last 6 to 8 months.

I learned how to make Chow Chow after I got married. Every year my mother-in-law would make up a big batch. Then my friend in Jones, Mrs. Crossley, would do the same. So I learned from the best!

Cornichon
(pronounced core-ne-shon)
Hot Pickled Cucumbers

10-12	small hot peppers
1	large cucumber, peeled
2	cups white vinegar

Wash hot peppers. Slice half of the peppers. Put all the peppers into a quart-size jar. Slice cucumber lengthwise into quarters and add to jar with peppers. Pour vinegar over vegetables to fill the jar. Refrigerate for at least 1 week before serving. Cut cucumbers into a dish and serve with stews, gumbos, sauce piquants, jambalayas, etc.

Diced peppered cucumbers complement any plate of food.

Chow Chow

1	large head cabbage, finely sliced and chopped
1	gallon cucumbers, finely chopped
2½	pounds bell peppers, finely chopped
½	gallon green tomatoes, finely chopped
6	medium onions, finely chopped
1½	quarts vinegar
4	cups sugar
1	small can dry yellow mustard
½	teaspoon ground cloves
½	tablespoon turmeric
1	tablespoon mustard seed

Combine all ingredients and let stand overnight. The following day, cook mixture until clear. Transfer mixture to sterilized jars and seal. Store in pantry and enjoy with meals.

Bourboned Sweet Potatoes

6   medium-size sweet potatoes, unpeeled
1   stick butter
½   cup bourbon
1½   cups light brown sugar

Cook potatoes in boiling water until barely tender. Peel and cut into fairly thick slices. Use some of butter to grease a baking dish. Place potato slices in baking dish. Pour bourbon over potatoes and dot with remaining butter. Sprinkle the brown sugar over all. Bake at 325 degrees for 30 to 40 minutes or until browned.

The flavor of this dish is great. I guess the bourbon does it! Actually, it does cook out (the alcohol), but the delicious taste of sweet potatoes is enhanced by the liquor. This is always a treat and a big success at dinners.

Thibodaux's Asparagus and Mushrooms

2   tablespoons butter
4   medium mushrooms, thinly sliced
¼   cup finely chopped onions
1   tablespoon chopped garlic
1   15 ounce can drained asparagus
     salt and pepper to taste

Melt butter in a saucepan. Sauté mushrooms, onions and garlic in butter until tender. Add asparagus and salt and pepper. Cook and gently stir until asparagus is hot. Serve immediately.

Missey recently cooked this dish. It is different. I love canned asparagus and it is better than simply pouring them out of the can onto the table. The recipe was given to Missey by a friend, Charollet Thibodaux.

Salsa Recipe 1

1   28 ounce can tomatoes, drained and chopped, or 5 large tomatoes, chopped

1   cup finely chopped onion

1   4 ounce can chopped green chiles, drained

1   tablespoon finely chopped canned jalapeño pepper

1   clove garlic, crushed

½   cup chopped bell pepper

2   tablespoons tomato paste

½   teaspoon salt

¼   teaspoon black pepper

¼   teaspoon chili powder

Combine all ingredients in a medium saucepan and stir well. Bring to a boil, stirring. Reduce heat and simmer 20 minutes, stirring occasionally. Cover and refrigerate 24 to 48 hours before serving. To serve, reheat over low heat, or serve cold. Makes 2½ cups.

Salsa Recipe 2

1   14.5 ounce can whole tomatoes, chopped

1   medium onion, chopped fine

¼   cup Galapagos, chopped fine or sliced thin

1   teaspoon oil

1   teaspoon vinegar

1   teaspoon minced garlic

½   teaspoon Accent

½   teaspoon ground cumin

Combine all ingredients.

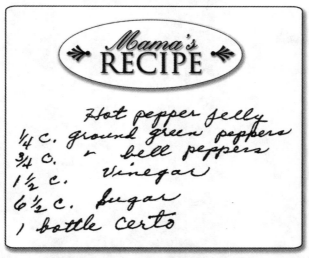

Mama's
RECIPE

Hot pepper jelly
1/4 c. ground green peppers
3/4 c. " bell peppers
1 1/2 c. Vinegar
6 1/2 c. Sugar
1 bottle Certo

More of Mama's time-tested recipes, and two of my favorites…even now!

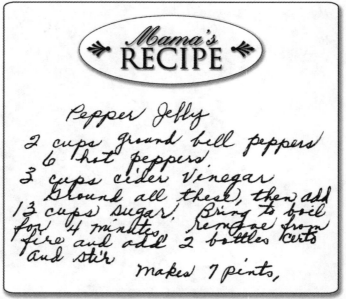

Mama's
RECIPE

Pepper Jelly
2 cups ground bell peppers
6 hot peppers
3 cups cider Vinegar
Ground all these, then add
13 cups sugar. Bring to boil
for 4 minutes, remove from
fire and add 2 bottles Certo
and stir
        makes 7 pints,

This recipe was the only pepper jelly recipe Mama ever made. We ate this with our meat, rice and gravy. I still enjoy pepper jelly today, especially with beef or mutton (but I cheat because I always have a good friend who supplies me with it.)

DESSERTS

SNACKS, COOKIES, CANDIES, CAKES & PIES

Alice and I had a busy day baking a bunch of her delicious pecan pies. She sends them out all over the United States — amazing that this happens in a small kitchen in Waterproof, Louisiana. I also learned how to make pralines that day — ate half of what I made!

Roasted Pecans

3	cups shelled pecans
	salt
½	stick margarine

For each 3 cups shelled pecans, melt ½ stick (¼ cup margarine) in shallow baking pan. Stir in pecans, coating with margarine, sprinkle with salt. Roast in slow oven, 275-300 degrees, for 45 minutes to an hour or until desired degree of toastiness is reached. Stir at about 15 minute intervals. When done, drain on absorbent paper. Be careful not to overcook. Smaller pecans toast faster. Also the amount of moisture in pecans affects cooking time.

For cocktail pecans: add ¼ cup Worcestershire sauce, 1 small, minced clove of garlic. Put in 250 degree oven until nuts absorb all liquid. Remove from oven, sprinkle salt and cayenne pepper as desired.

Store for about a year in airtight containers in the refrigerator or several years in the freezer.

Popcorn Balls

Recipe 1

1	cup cane syrup
	pinch of salt
½	tablespoon butter
1	gallon popped popcorn

Cook syrup and salt in a heavy saucepan until a drop forms a hard ball in a cup of cold water. Remove from heat, add butter and mix. Pour syrup in a thin stream over popcorn while stirring popcorn. Shape mixture into balls and place on waxed paper. Allow to cool. Store in an airtight container. Makes about 1 dozen.

Recipe 2

3	cups water
3	cups sugar
1	gallon popped popcorn

Cook water and sugar in a heavy saucepan until a drop forms a hard ball in a cup of cold water. Remove from heat. Pour syrup over popcorn while stirring popcorn. Form mixture into balls and place on waxed paper. Allow to cool. Store in an airtight container. Makes about 1 dozen.

Mama made a lot of popcorn balls while I was growing up. My favorite was sugar and water syrup balls. Sometimes she would not make balls with it but only let the corn and syrup cool in the pot. Then I would break off chunks to enjoy as soon as the mixture was cool enough.

My friend, Carol Elias, gave this recipe to me many years ago. I really enjoy this snack. I had never eaten this until I moved to northeast Louisiana — wonder why they named this Texas Trash?

Texas Trash

1	box Cheerios cereal
1	box Wheat Chex cereal
1	box Rice Chex cereal
1	package pretzels
1	tablespoon plus 1 teaspoon seasoned salt
1	tablespoon plus 1 teaspoon garlic salt
1	tablespoon plus 1 teaspoon celery salt
1	tablespoon plus 1 teaspoon black pepper
1	tablespoon plus 1 teaspoon chili powder
2	sticks butter or margarine, cut into chunks
¼	cup Worcestershire sauce
	pecans and/or peanuts (optional)

Pour cereals and pretzels into a large pan. Combine seasoned salt, garlic salt, celery salt, black pepper and chili powder and sprinkle over chunks of butter. Distribute seasoned butter chunks throughout cereal mixture. Sprinkle with Worcestershire sauce. Bake mixture at 225 degrees for 2 to 4 hours or until crisp, stirring occasionally. Halfway through cooking, add nuts, if desired. Cool mixture before storing in an airtight container. This makes tons but can be kept a long time.

got this recipe from one of my dear nieces, Jan. She is a very good cook also and cooks for many occasions. This is good for parties and large family gatherings. Jan made this recipe when RFD-TV had the launching party on DirecTV and it definitely was a big hit.

Cheese Ball à Jan

3	8 ounce packages cream cheese, softened
1	5 ounce can chopped olives
1	4 ounce can chopped mushrooms
1	5 ounce jar dried beef, chopped
1	large bunch green onions, chopped
½	teaspoon Accent

Combine all ingredients together and mix thoroughly. Roll mixture into a ball and serve with crackers. Makes 1 large ball.

Sweet Potato Cheese Ball

1   roll smoked cheese, room temperature

1   pound mild Cheddar cheese, shredded, room temperature

1   8 ounce package cream cheese, room temperature

1   cup mashed cooked sweet potatoes

1   teaspoon Worcestershire sauce

1   teaspoon garlic powder

1   cup finely chopped pecans

Combine all ingredients except pecans. Divide mixture in half and shape into 2 balls. Roll balls in pecans. Cover and chill overnight.

My friend, Edwina Harper, has taught me how to make many sweet potato dishes. She and her husband raise sweet potatoes so it was as natural for her to use her commodity as it is for me to use rice!

This is a great recipe when expecting a lot of children to appear for a treat. I would call it "my easy sugar yam cookie." I treat myself with these also.

I always liked to cook but cookie baking wasn't my favorite thing to do in the kitchen. However, I made these cookies for cooking projects in Home Economics in high school. I enjoyed baking these and more so enjoyed eating them.

Easy Yam Cookies

3	sticks butter, softened
3	cups sugar
3	eggs, beaten
6	cups flour
3	tablespoons baking powder
3	cups cooked yams
1	tablespoon vanilla
1½	teaspoons salt

Combine all ingredients and mix well. Drop mixture by teaspoonfuls onto baking sheets. Bake at 350 degrees until bottoms of cookies are golden brown. Makes about 210 cookies.

Sugar Cookies

2¼	cups flour
1½	teaspoons baking powder
¼	teaspoon salt
½	teaspoon nutmeg
1½	teaspoons lemon zest
½	cup butter or shortening, softened
2	eggs, well beaten
	sugar for sprinkling

Sift together flour, baking powder, salt and nutmeg. Set aside. In a separate bowl, cream together lemon zest and butter. Beat in eggs. Gradually blend in dry ingredients. Chill dough until firm enough to roll. Roll dough to ⅛-inch thick. Cut dough with a cookie cutter and sprinkle with sugar. Transfer to an ungreased baking sheet. Bake at 400 degrees for 10 minutes. Makes 3 dozen.

Coconut Macaroons

1   3½ ounce jar flaked coconut
3   egg whites
¾   cup sugar
3   tablespoons flour
½   teaspoon vanilla

Combine coconut, egg whites and sugar in a saucepan. Cook over medium heat, stirring constantly, for 8 to 10 minutes or until mixture is thick and looks like mashed potatoes. Do not boil! Remove from heat. Stir in flour and vanilla. Drop onto 2 greased and lightly floured baking sheets and let stand at room temperature for about 1 hour. Bake at 300 degrees for 22 to 25 minutes. Makes 24 cookies.

I have used this recipe since 1956. These are my favorite cookies.

Oatmeal Cookies

1   cup shortening
1   cup brown sugar
1   cup granulated sugar
2   eggs, beaten
1   teaspoon vanilla
1½   cups sifted flour
1   teaspoon salt
1   teaspoon baking powder or soda
3   cups dry quick oats
½   cup nuts

Cream shortening and sugars. Beat in eggs and vanilla. Blend in flour, salt and baking powder. Stir in oats and nuts. Roll dough into logs and place on waxed paper. Chill several hours. Slice into rounds and place on ungreased baking sheets. Bake at 350 degrees for 8 to 10 minutes.

I made these many, many times while in Home Economics. I still do as well as the chocolate chip ones (which are my favorite because of the chocolate.

German Cookies

6	cups flour
1½	tablespoons cinnamon
¼	teaspoon freshly ground nutmeg
¼	teaspoon salt
4	sticks butter, softened
2	cups sugar
2	eggs
½	cup white wine
1	egg, lightly beaten
½	cup sugar

Mix flour, cinnamon, nutmeg and salt in a bowl. In a separate bowl, beat butter with an electric mixer until softened. Add 2 cups sugar and beat until light and fluffy. Beat in 2 eggs, one at a time. Alternately, beat in dry ingredients and wine, using about one-third of each at a time. Dough will be very soft. Divide dough into 5 equal parts. Flatten and wrap each in plastic wrap. Refrigerate dough overnight.

Roll out dough to about ¼-inch thick on a lightly floured board. Cut with a cookie cutter and place on greased baking sheets. Brush tops of cookies with lightly beaten egg and sprinkle with ¼ cup sugar. Bake at 350 degrees for 18 to 20 minutes or until golden brown. Transfer to a wire rack to cool completely. Makes 5 to 6 dozen cookies.

Cookies are even better after being stored in a cookie jar for one week.

Best-Ever Chocolate Chip Cookies

1½	cups sifted all-purpose flour
1	teaspoon baking soda
1	teaspoon cinnamon
2	sticks butter, softened
½	cup light brown sugar
1	cup granulated sugar
1	egg
1	teaspoon vanilla
1½	cups old-fashioned rolled oats
1	cup semi-sweet chocolate chips

Combine flour, baking soda and cinnamon in a bowl. In a separate bowl, cream butter and sugars using an electric mixer on medium speed until light and fluffy. Beat in egg and vanilla. Reduce speed to low and blend in dry ingredients. Fold in oats and chocolate chips. Cover with plastic wrap and chill 1 hour.

Shape dough into 1-inch balls and place 2 inches apart on 2 greased baking sheets. Flatten each cookie slightly. Bake at 350 degrees for 10 to 12 minutes or until cookies are lightly browned around edges. Cool baking sheets slightly on wire racks. Remove cookies from baking sheets and cool completely on wire racks. Makes 4 dozen cookies.

Heavenly Hash

2	cups sugar
1	cup milk
1	12 ounce package chocolate chips
1	teaspoon vanilla
1½	cups pecans, chopped
1	(10 ounce) bag miniature marshmallows

Combine sugar and milk in a saucepan. Bring to a boil and boil 5 minutes. Remove from heat. Drop in chocolate chips and vanilla. Beat well until chips melt. Add pecans. Pour half the mixture into a dish. Top with marshmallows. Pour remainder of chocolate mixture over marshmallows. Allow to cool completely in refrigerator. Cut into squares.

Verda's Pralines

1	cup granulated sugar
1	cup brown sugar
¾	cup milk
2	cups pecans
1	tablespoon butter
1	teaspoon vanilla
1	pinch baking soda

Mix sugars and milk in a large saucepan. Boil mixture until a drop forms a ball in cold water. Add pecans, butter, vanilla and baking soda. Remove from heat and beat until mixture becomes shiny and glossy. Drop mixture by tablespoonfuls onto waxed paper. Cool. Store in an airtight container.

I make only a small batch because it is easier to beat.

Max Dollar's Buttermilk Candy

2 **cups sugar**
½ **teaspoon baking soda**
3 **tablespoons light corn syrup**
4 **tablespoons margarine or butter**
1 **cup buttermilk**
1 **teaspoon vanilla**
2 **cups pecans**

Combine sugar, baking soda, corn syrup, margarine and buttermilk in a large saucepan over medium-high heat. Bring to a boil, stirring sides and bottom to prevent burning. Boil for about 2 minutes. Reduce heat to medium-low. Cook until a drop forms a firm ball in cold water. Remove from heat and cool. Beat in vanilla and pecans. Pour mixture over waxed paper. When cool, cut into squares. Enjoy!

My neighbor, Don, brought me a batch of candy which Mr. Max Dollar had made. Max would make this candy for his friends and acquaintances. It was the best candy I had ever eaten. So, naturally, I asked for Max's recipe. Max is deceased now, but I feel like he and his candy will live forever!

Whiskey Balls

1 **cup ground vanilla wafers**
¼ **cup whiskey or rum (optional)**
1 **cup pecans, ground**
2 **tablespoons light corn syrup**
1 **tablespoon cocoa powder**
⅓ **cup powdered sugar**

Mix together all ingredients except powdered sugar. Form mixture into balls. Roll balls in powdered sugar. Store in an airtight container.

I usually make these at Christmas. You may choose to make these and omit the liquor. I have been using this recipe since 1976 because it is exactly how Mama made her whiskey balls.

Chocolate Balls

1	stick butter or margarine
1	14 ounce can sweetened condensed milk
2	1 pound packages powdered sugar, divided
1	quart finely chopped pecans
1	16 ounce package chocolate chips
¾	block paraffin wax

In a double boiler, mix butter and milk. Heat slightly. Add 1¾ pounds powdered sugar and mix well. Stir in pecans. Remove from heat and cool. Use a teaspoon to form mixture into small balls. Roll balls in remaining powdered sugar and place in a pan. Stick a toothpick into each ball. Freeze 2 hours.

Melt chocolate chips and paraffin wax together in the top of double boiler one hour before using. Dip frozen balls in chocolate mixture and cool. Remove toothpicks and store in an airtight container in the refrigerator.

5-Minute Fudge

⅔	cup evaporated milk
1⅔	cups sugar
1½	cups diced marshmallows (about 16)
1½	cups chocolate chips (about 9 ounces)
1	teaspoon vanilla
½	cup chopped pecans or almonds

Mix evaporated milk and sugar in a saucepan. Bring to a boil and cook 5 minutes, stirring constantly. Remove from heat. Add in marshmallows, chocolate chips, vanilla and nuts. Stir 1 to 2 minutes or until marshmallows melt. Pour mixture into a greased 9-inch square pan. Cool and cut into squares.

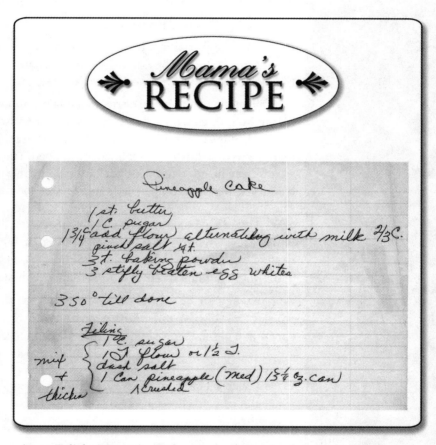

Pineapple Cake

1 st. butter
1 C. sugar
1 3/4 C add flour — alternating with milk 2/3 C.
pinch salt 1/4 t.
3 t. baking powder
3 stifly beaten egg whites

350° till done

Filing
1 C. sugar
1 T flour or 1 1/2 T.
dash salt
mix 1 Can pineapple (med) 15 1/4 oz. can
      crushed
+
thicken

Aunt Edith, Mama's sister, made this cake for us. So Mama
had her recipe in my file box. It is the best I ever ate!

Successful Cheesecakes

There's something irresistible about cheesecake. Rich, creamy and satin smooth, it is one of the best-loved desserts of all time.

The techniques for making luscious cheesecakes are simple to master. Follow the instructions carefully, pay attention to the details and even if you are a novice baker you can make an impressive cheesecake on the very first try.

Preparation

Before you begin baking, be sure all the ingredients are at room temperature. They will mix more easily and the finished cake will have a smoother texture.

Combine the cream cheese or ricotta and eggs thoroughly before adding any liquid extracts, heavy cream or sour cream. Lumps are impossible to remove once the liquid ingredients that thin the batter have been added. The paddle attachment of an electric mixer is ideal for mixing the batter. Regular whipping beaters incorporate too much air into the batter, which can lead to cracks in the finished cake. Also, if too much air is worked into the batter, the cake will be less creamy. If you must use regular whipping beaters, set the mixer at low or medium-low speed so only a minimum amount of air is whipped into the batter.

Fold in whipped cream and beaten egg whites with a wire whisk or a rubber spatula. Fold gently and slowly, taking care not to deflate the volume of the whipped ingredients.

Cream Cheese

Cream cheese comes in many different varieties. Always use regular cream cheese for cheesecakes, unless the recipe says otherwise.

Base Ingredients

Cheesecake bases are generally made from cookie crumbs mixed with softened or melted butter. Although many recipes call for graham cracker crumbs, almost any cookie will do, including cream-filled sandwich cookies. To crush the cookies, either grind them in a food processor fitted with a metal blade, or place them in a plastic bag and crush them with a rolling pin.

What Went Wrong?

Cracks in the surface can occur because cheesecakes release a considerable amount of steam while they bake and during cooling time. Too much steam released too quickly causes the cheesecake to crack.

Extremes of temperature can also lead to surface cracks. That is why baking temperatures for cheesecakes are relatively low, and bakers are warned not to set cheesecakes in cold or drafty places to cool. If possible, cool the cheesecake in a turned-off oven. Use a wooden spoon to keep the door slightly ajar.

Deep cracks mean the egg white structure has collapsed. The cheesecake will be wet, more like a pudding than a cake.

Shallow cracks often occur despite all efforts to prevent them. Accept them as part of a cheesecake's home-baked charm or cover them with fruit.

Step By Step

1 Grease the bottom and sides of a springform pan. Combine crumbs with butter and sugar and press evenly into the bottom and up sides of the pan. In warm weather, refrigerate the pan until ready to use.

2 Use the paddle attachment of an electric mixer to beat the cream cheese smooth before adding any other ingredients. Regular whipping beaters can lead to cracks in the surface of the finished cake.

3 To ensure that the batter has no lumps and no ingredients stuck to the bottom of the bowl, stop the mixer several times while making the batter and scrape down the paddle and sides of the bowl.

4 Pour the batter into the prepared pan and set the pan on a baking sheet. Bake as directed. Cover with aluminum foil partway through baking if the top browns too quickly.

5 The finished cheesecake will have a dull, not shiny, finish. The center should be soft, but it should not wobble. Run a knife around the sides of the cooled cake to loosen it from the pan.

6 Release the spring and remove the pan sides. Leave the cake on the pan bottom for serving. Decorate with fresh fruit or sour cream, or serve plain.

This is my family's favorite cheesecake. I got the recipe from Nelda Johnson many years ago. I had misplaced the original recipe but managed to retrieve it from another friend, Beverly McCormack. Both ladies have moved away since we all shared this recipe.

Cheesecake

Batter

2	8 ounce packages cream cheese, softened
2-3	eggs
⅔	cup sugar
1	teaspoon vanilla
1	graham cracker or pastry pie crust, unbaked
1	cup sour cream
1	teaspoon vanilla
2	tablespoons sugar

Fruit Topping

1	16 ounce can cherries, drained, juice reserved, or frozen strawberries
2	tablespoons sugar
2	teaspoons cornstarch
	red food coloring

Combine cream cheese, 2 eggs, ⅔ cup sugar and 1 teaspoon vanilla in a bowl. Use an electric mixer to beat until smooth. If batter is not thin enough to pour, beat in 1 extra egg. Pour batter into unbaked pie crust. Bake at 375 degrees for 20 minutes. Cool 15 minutes. Combine sour cream, 1 teaspoon vanilla and 2 tablespoons sugar. Pour mixture over cooled layer. Bake at 425 degrees for 10 minutes longer. Chill overnight. Serve plain or with fruit topping.

To make topping, blend ½ cup reserved juice, sugar and cornstarch in a saucepan. Cook, stirring constantly, until thickened and clear. Stir in a few drops of food coloring. Add 1 cup of canned cherries. Cool before spooning over cheesecake.

Cajun Cream Cake

Batter

2	cups sugar
½	cup shortening
½	cup corn oil
5	eggs, separated
2	cups flour
1	cup buttermilk
1	teaspoon baking soda
1	3½ ounce can flake coconut
1½	cups chopped pecans
1	teaspoon vanilla

Icing

1	8 ounce package cream cheese, softened
1	stick margarine, softened
1	16 ounce package powdered sugar
1½	cups granulated sugar
1	teaspoon vanilla

This is a very special cake as a special niece, Deborah, gave me the recipe. And it is the ultimate! She has shared her red velvet cake with me but I really prefer this one! It is pretty to serve and real tasty!

Cream together sugar, shortening and oil. Add egg yolks, one at a time, and beat well. Add flour, buttermilk, baking soda, coconut, pecans and vanilla. Mix well. Beat egg whites until stiff. Fold whites into batter. Divide batter among three 9 inch cake pans. Bake at 350 degrees for 25 minutes. Remove from oven and cool 5 minutes. Invert cake layers onto dinner plates and remove pans. Cool.

Mix together all icing ingredients. Spread icing over each cake layer. Stack layers and spread icing on the sides of cake.

Angel Cake

1	angel food cake, or 1 package angel food cake mix, prepared as directed on package
1	8 ounce package cream cheese, softened
½	cup sugar
¼	cup lemon juice
1	14 ounce can sweetened condensed milk
1	8 ounce container Cool Whip, thawed
1	10 ounce package frozen strawberries, thawed

Cut angel food cake into small pieces. Mix together cream cheese, sugar, lemon juice and condensed milk. Fold in Cool Whip and strawberries. Layer cake pieces and strawberry mixture in a 9x13 inch pan. Refrigerate.

High School Brownies

½	cup shortening or butter
½	teaspoon vanilla
1	cup sugar
2	eggs
2	ounces (2 squares) unsweetened chocolate, melted
1	cup flour
1	teaspoon baking powder
¼	teaspoon salt
¾	cup chopped pecans
	light chocolate frosting

Cream shortening. Beat in vanilla. Add sugar and beat. Beat in eggs. Add chocolate and mix. Sift together flour, baking powder and salt. Add dry ingredients to creamed mixture. Stir in pecans. Pour batter into a baking pan sprayed with Pam. Bake at 375 degrees for 20 to 35 minutes or until done. Ice with light chocolate frosting.

Special Brownies

Layer 1

3	cups sugar
6	sticks butter, softened
6	eggs
1	teaspoon vanilla
½	cup cocoa
2	cups self-rising flour

Layer 2

1¾	cups sugar
3	8 ounce packages cream cheese, softened
3	eggs
¾	cup self-rising flour

For first layer, cream sugar and butter. Add eggs, vanilla, cocoa and flour. Pour batter into a greased or sprayed 11x17 inch pan.

For second layer, cream sugar, cream cheese, eggs and flour. Dot spoonfuls of second layer on top of first layer. Cut through batter with a knife to swirl. Bake at 350 degrees for 30 to 35 minutes or until done.

Brownies usually are very popular at family outings, dinners and even socials. My friend from New Orleans bakes these often as they are so quick and easy. Lucy Suzanne loves them because they don't have nuts inside (plus she loves chocolate as much as her grandmother.)

My friend, Gail, cele-
brated my 60th birthday
with me. She made my
day when she came
over to ease my pain. I
was very upset about
being that old and told
her I wanted to be 30
again. So without my
knowing what her plans
were, she presented me
with half of my birth-
day cake which was
symbolic of me only being
30. We really enjoyed the
day and the cake was
delicious!

Gail's Mama's Pecan Cake

Cake

1	18 ounce box yellow cake mix
3½-4 cups ground pecans	
1	12 ounce can evaporated milk
4	tablespoons margarine or butter
1	teaspoon vanilla nut flavoring
1-1½ cups sugar, according to your taste	

7-Minute Frosting

2	egg whites
1½	cups sugar
	dash of salt
⅓	cup water
2	teaspoons light corn syrup
1	teaspoon vanilla

Prepare cake mix according to directions on package. Bake in 2 layers and cool. Split each layer in half horizontally, resulting in 4 layers. Combine pecans, evaporated milk, margarine, flavoring and sugar in a saucepan. Cook over medium heat, stirring often, until thick enough for a filling. Cool. Stack cake layers, spreading filling between layers. Frost top and sides of cake with 7-Minute Frosting.

To make frosting, combine all ingredients in the top of a double boiler. Stir until well mixed. Place over boiling water. Beat constantly with an electric mixer until stiff peaks form. Beat by hand until frosting reaches a spreading consistency.

Mama always had thicker filling than cake layers.

Strawberry 'n Cream Shortcakes

2	pints whole strawberries, hulled and rinsed, divided
½	cup granulated sugar
1	tablespoon fresh lemon juice
1	cup heavy whipping cream
2	tablespoons powdered sugar
3	tablespoons sour cream
1	teaspoon vanilla
	Cream Shortcakes (recipe below)

In a large bowl, combine 1 pint strawberries and granulated sugar. Crush berries. Slice remaining pint of strawberries, reserving 4 to 6 whole berries to use for garnish. Stir sliced berries into crushed berry mixture. Mix in lemon juice. Refrigerate 1 hour.

In another large bowl, beat cream and powdered sugar until soft peaks form. Add sour cream and vanilla and beat until stiff.

Split cream shortcakes in half horizontally. Place bottom halves on individual dessert plates. Spoon strawberry mixture and 1½ cups cream mixture evenly among cake bottoms. Replace cake tops and dollop remaining cream mixture on top of each. Garnish with reserved strawberries.

Cream Shortcakes

1	cup flour
1	cup cake flour
3	tablespoons sugar
1	tablespoon baking powder
¼	teaspoon salt
1	stick butter, cut into pieces
1	cup plus 1 tablespoon heavy whipping cream, divided

Combine flours, sugar, baking powder and salt. Cut in butter pieces with a pastry blender or 2 table knives until mixture resembles coarse crumbs. Gradually add 1 cup cream, tossing with a fork until dough is evenly moistened. Transfer dough to a work area and knead gently until dough just holds together. Roll or pat dough to ½ inch thick. Cut dough into circles using a 3 inch cutter. Place circles on a well-greased or foil-lined baking sheet. Brush tops with remaining 1 tablespoon cream. Bake at 400 degrees for 18 to 20 minutes or until tops are golden brown. Cool.

Every time I eat at a Piccadilly Cafeteria, I enjoy a strawberry shortcake. Now I make my own at home. These are like cake shortcakes, but they are the original shortcakes and equally as good. A friend of mine, Mick, loves these and even eats them for breakfast.

Baked Apples

6-8	large cooking apples
2-3	cups sugar, depending on tartness of apples
¼	cup flour
	butter or margarine
1½-2	teaspoons cinnamon
1	cup chopped walnuts
1	cup miniature marshmallows, more if desired
2	tablespoons vanilla
¼	cup raisins
2½	cups water

Cut unpeeled apples in half and remove cores. Place apples, cut-side up, in a 9x13 inch baking pan. Mix sugar and flour and sprinkle evenly over apples. Place 1 teaspoon butter in each apple cavity. Sprinkle with cinnamon, walnuts and marshmallows. Pour water into pan without pouring over apples. Drop raisins into water and add vanilla to water. Bake at 350 degrees until apples are tender. (If some flour remains on top, just spoon a little of cooking liquid over top.)

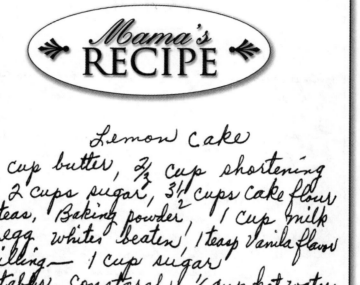

Lemon Cake

⅓ cup butter, ⅔ cup shortening
2 cups sugar, 3½ cups cake flour
2 teas. Baking powder, 1 cup milk
6 egg whites beaten, 1 teasp Vanila flavor
Filling — 1 cup sugar
3 tabls. Constarch, ½ cup hot water
⅔ stick butter or oleo
     Grated rind of 2 lemons
6 egg yolk
Juice of 2 lemons

This recipe is an "oldie" but a "goodie." I never was as good
a cake baker as my aunts were.

Banana Cake

½ cup Crisco
1½ cup sugar
2 eggs
2 cups flour
½ teaspoon salt

¾ teaspoon Soda
¾ cup Buttermilk
1 cup mashed Bananas
1 teaspoon Vanila
1 cup pecans

mix

Cream Crisco and sugar, then add eggs. Sift soda, salt, flour, and add alternately with milk. Add Bananas, nuts and Vanila. Pour into greased and floured pans. Bake in moderate (350°F) oven about 25 to 30 minutes

Filling

Combine 1 cup Sugar, 1 cup evaporated milk and 3 eggs yolk, and cook until thickened. Remove from heat and add 1 can coconut, 1 cup nuts, and 1 teaspoon Vanila.
Spread between layers and cover top of cake

Mama did not like to bake but when she did, this was usually the cake of her choice. Her sisters were great cake bakers, especially Aunt Edith. This was about the only cake that Mama liked to bake. I found her original hand written recipe in my old recipe file (it was written in her own handwriting on an old sheet of paper which had yellowed.)

Whipped Cream Frosting

2   cups heavy whipping cream
2   tablespoons powdered sugar
1   teaspoon vanilla

Process all ingredients until firm peaks form.

Chocolate Butter Cream Frosting

3   stick butter or margarine, softened
4   cups powdered sugar
¼   cup cocoa
2   tablespoons milk
1   teaspoon vanilla

Process butter and half of powdered sugar until creamy.
Add remaining powdered sugar and cocoa. Process until
light and fluffy, stopping to scrape down sides of bowl as
needed. Add milk and vanilla and process until mixture is
a spreading consistency.

For plain vanilla frosting, prepare as directed above, omit-
ting cocoa.

Peanut Butter Filling

4	tablespoons butter or margarine, softened
1½	cups powdered sugar
¼	cup creamy peanut butter
1½	tablespoons milk
1	teaspoon vanilla

Process butter and half of powdered sugar until creamy. Add remaining powdered sugar, peanut butter, milk and vanilla. Process until mixture is smooth, stopping once to scrape down sides of processor bowl. For a 3 layer cake, double recipe.

Mint-Cream Filling

1	cup heavy whipping cream
2-3	drops green food coloring
2	tablespoons powdered sugar
¼	teaspoon peppermint extract

Process cream and food coloring in a food processor until foamy. Gradually add powdered sugar, processing until soft peaks form. Stir in peppermint extract.

Two tablespoons crème de menthe may be substituted for food coloring and peppermint extract.

Sweet Potato Cake

Batter

1	cup shortening or butter
2	cups sugar
4	eggs
1	cup cooked and mashed sweet potatoes
2½	cups cake flour
2½	teaspoons baking powder
½	cup milk
1	teaspoon vanilla
1	teaspoon coconut flavoring
1	teaspoon vinegar
1	cup nuts
½	cup coconut

Icing

4	tablespoons butter, softened
1	1 pound package powdered sugar
	evaporated milk
¼	cup chopped pecans
¼	cup raisins

Cream together shortening and sugar. Beat in eggs, one at a time. Add mashed potatoes. Blend in flour, baking powder, milk, vanilla, coconut flavoring, vinegar, nuts and coconut. Pour batter into a greased and floured Bundt pan. Bake at 350 degrees for 35 to 40 minutes.

For icing, mix butter, powdered sugar and enough milk to reach a spreading consistency. Spread over cake. Sprinkle pecans and raisins on top.

Classic CAJUN DEUX

This is an old one from my high school days. I seldom bake a sweet potato cake because we usually eat them baked and there are none left over to use in another recipe.

This cake is awesome! The wire cake racks are great to use (something I never had until a couple years ago.) The wax paper keeps the cake from having ridges across the layers. Hopefully the layers won't stick to the wax paper! I usually make this cake when I want to make a good impression!

Nutty Praline Cake

Cake

1	cup brown sugar
1	stick butter or margarine
¼	cup heavy whipping cream
¼	cup pecans, chopped fine
½	teaspoon vanilla
1	box caramel cake mix
3	eggs
1⅓	cups water
⅓	cup vegetable oil

Combine brown sugar, butter and cream in a small heavy saucepan. Cook over medium-low heat, stirring constantly, until butter melts and mixture is well blended. Stir in pecans and vanilla. Pour mixture into 2 round cake pans which have been sprayed with Pam. In a large bowl, combine cake mix, eggs, water and oil. Beat with an electric mixer on medium speed for 2 minutes. Slowly pour batter over pecan mixture. Bake at 325 degrees for 30 to 35 minutes. Cool in pans 5 minutes. Invert onto wax paper on wire racks and cool completely.

To assemble, stack cake layers with pecan praline layers up. Spread icing between layers and over top of cake. Store in an airtight container in the refrigerator.

Icing

1	8 ounce package cream cheese, softened
¼	cup plus 2 tablespoons milk
4	cups powdered sugar
¼	cup butterscotch chips, melted

For icing, beat cream cheese and milk in a medium bowl until well blended. Gradually add powdered sugar and beat until smooth. Add melted butterscotch chips and beat until blended.

Praline Syrup

4   tablespoons butter
½   cup brown sugar
¼   cup heavy whipping cream
2   tablespoons light corn syrup
¼   cup finely chopped pecans
1   teaspoon vanilla

Melt butter over low heat in a heavy saucepan. Add sugar, cream and corn syrup. Cook and stir until sugar is dissolved and mixture is smooth. Stir in pecans and cook over medium heat, stirring constantly, for 3 minutes. Remove from heat and stir in vanilla.

This is my favorite syrup, which I use to top ice cream, cheesecakes or cakes. Anything I want to give a dignified taste to. What a treat!

Almond Joy Cake

1   18 ounce box chocolate cake mix
½   cup evaporated milk
½   cup sugar
24   large marshmallows
1   14 ounce package coconut
½   cup sugar
½   cup evaporated milk
4   tablespoons margarine
1   10 ounce package chocolate chips
1   cup almonds, divided

Prepare and bake cake according to package directions in a 9x13 inch baking pan. Mix ½ cup milk and ½ cup milk in a saucepan. Bring to a boil. Remove from heat and stir in marshmallows until melted. Add coconut and spread over warm cake. In a clean saucepan, place ½ cup sugar, ½ cup milk and margarine. Bring to a boil. Remove from heat and stir in chocolate chips until smooth. Add ¾ cup almonds and spread over coconut layer. Sprinkle remaining ¼ cup almonds on top. Cool completely before cutting.

Almond Joy candy is my most favorite candy. So now I enjoy this cake as much! It is the ultimate with coconut and chocolate!

I don't know where I got this recipe. It is one I've had for many years. What I like about it is that it is so different. It is really good at holidays.

Gumdrop Cake

8	ounces gumdrops, each cut into thirds
8	ounces seedless white raisins
8	ounces nuts of your choice (mine is pecans)
¼	cup flour
2	cups flour
½	teaspoon salt
½	teaspoon baking soda
½	teaspoon cinnamon
⅛	teaspoon cloves
⅛	teaspoon nutmeg
½	cup shortening
1	cup sugar
½	teaspoon vanilla
1	egg
¾	cup sweetened applesauce
½	cup hot water

Mix gumdrops, raisins and nuts. Stir in ¼ cup flour to coat. Set aside. In another bowl, sift together 2 cups flour, salt, baking soda, cinnamon, cloves and nutmeg. Set aside. In a large bowl, cream shortening, sugar and vanilla. Add egg and beat well. Mix together applesauce and hot water. Add dry ingredients to creamed mixture alternately with thinned applesauce, beginning and ending with dry ingredients. Stir in candy mixture. Pour batter into a 9x5 inch loaf pan lined with heavy parchment paper (wax paper can be substituted.) Bake at 325 degrees for 1½ to 1¾ hours. Cool. Remove from pan and wrap in foil.

Crêpes Fitzgerald

4   eggs
¼   teaspoon salt
2   cups flour
2¼   cups milk
4   tablespoons butter, melted
1   pint heavy whipping cream, whipped, for
       topping

Beat together eggs and salt in a medium mixing bowl. Gradually add flour and milk, alternately, beating until smooth. Beat in melted butter. Refrigerate at least 1 hour. Pour a small amount of batter in a crêpe pan or in a small skillet. Cook until sides begin to curl. Flip over and cook briefly. Remove from heat and place in a flat pan or baking sheet. Working with one crêpe at a time, place each crêpe on a flat surface. Spoon 1 to 2 tablespoons filling into each crêpe and roll like a cigar. Serve topped with whipped cream. Makes 3 dozen.

Crêpe Filling

1   8 ounce package cream cheese, softened
¾   cup sour cream
6   tablespoons sugar
2   teaspoons lemon zest
2   teaspoons orange zest
       juice of 1 lemon
3   cups sliced strawberries

Beat together cream cheese, sour cream, sugar and zests with an electric mixer. Fold in strawberries. Fills 36 crêpes.

I had always eaten these at restaurants. However, I got hands on experience when I went to Oslo, Norway. I worked with the pastry chef, who spoke no English. But we got along real well. I taught the chefs my Cajun recipes and I got to make (and eat) their cooking. In the meantime, I learned how to prepare these delicious crêpes!

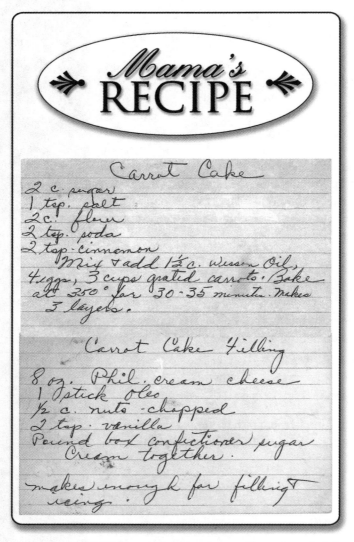

Mama's RECIPE

Carrot Cake

2 c. sugar
1 tsp. salt
2 c. flour
2 tsp. soda
2 tsp. cinnamon
    Mix & add 1½ c. Wesson Oil,
4 eggs, 3 cups grated carrots. Bake
at 350° for 30-35 minutes. Makes
3 layers.

Carrot Cake Filling

8 oz. Phil. cream cheese
1 stick oleo
½ c. nuts - chopped
2 tsp. vanilla
Pound box confectioner sugar
    Cream together.

makes enough for filling &
icing.

Mama didn't like carrots but she really enjoyed this cake. She usually drank her strong coffee with it.

Vanilla Wafer Cake

2   cups sugar

2   sticks butter or margarine, softened

6   eggs

1   12 ounce box vanilla wafers, crushed

½   cup milk

1   7 ounce can flaked coconut

1   cup pecans

Cream together sugar and butter. Add eggs, one at a time, beating well after each addition. Add crushed wafers and milk. Stir in coconut and pecans. Pour batter into a greased and floured 10 inch tube pan. Bake at 275 degrees for 1 hour, 15 minutes. Cool before inverting onto a cake plate. Serve with Cool Whip or whipped cream.

My sister-in-law, Ollie Marie, served this cake with one of her delicious meals. So I just had to have her recipe. She is a great cook!

Mama's RECIPE

Coffee Lemon cake
1 box Duncan Hines white cake mix
4 eggs
1 box Lemon jello, gelatin
¾ cup crisco oil
¾ cup apricot nectar
1 Tablespoon flavor
Put all together, Beat it,
Topping – 1 cup powdered sugar
to spreading consistancy

Mama usually served this cake when she and her neighbor, Mamie, visited. They enjoyed each other's company as well as the cake and coffee.

This is also a must in the morning. I remember the aroma but I cannot remember the rest of the topping ingredients. I think it was milk added to the powdered sugar. You can use your own imagination.

Orange-Glazed Coffee Cake

Dough

1	package active dry yeast
¼	cup warm water (105 to 115 degrees)
½	cup warm milk (105 to 115 degrees)
½	cup freshly squeezed orange juice
½	cup sugar
½	cup ricotta cheese
1	tablespoon orange zest
½	teaspoon salt
1	egg, lightly beaten
3½-4	cups all-purpose flour

Glaze

1	egg, lightly beaten

Icing

1	cup powdered sugar
1½-2	tablespoons freshly squeezed orange juice

Dissolve yeast in warm water in a large mixing bowl. Let stand 5 to 10 minutes or until foamy. Stir in milk, orange juice, sugar, cheese, orange zest, salt and egg. Using an electric mixer with a paddle attachment and set on low speed, beat 2 cups flour into yeast mixture until a wet dough forms. Beat in remaining flour, ½ cup at a time, until a stiff dough forms. Turn dough out onto a lightly floured surface and knead 5 to 10 minutes or until smooth and elastic, adding more flour as needed to prevent sticking. Place dough in a large greased bowl, turning to coat. Cover loosely with a damp cloth. Let rise in a warm place for 1½ hours or until doubled in bulk. Punch dough and turn onto a lightly floured surface. Knead 1 to 2 minutes. Divide dough into 3 equal sections. Roll each section into a 20 inch long rope. Braid ropes together. Coil braided dough in a greased 10 inch springform pan. Cover loosely with a damp cloth and let rise in a warm place 30 minutes or until almost doubled in size.

(continued on next page)

Orange-Glazed Coffee Cake *(continued)*

Brush dough with beaten egg for a glaze. Bake at 425 degrees for 25 to 30 minutes or until golden brown. Turn cake out onto a wire rack to cool slightly.

For icing, stir together powdered sugar and orange juice until smooth. Spread icing over warm cake. Serve warm. Serves 12.

German Chocolate Brownie Cheesecake

Brownie Crust

1	18 ounce box German chocolate cake mix
⅔	cup butter, softened
½	cup shredded coconut
1	egg

Filling

1	8 ounce package cream cheese, softened
2	eggs
¾	cup sugar
2	teaspoons vanilla

Topping

2	cups sour cream
¼	cup sugar
1	tablespoon vanilla

A friend of mine, Jodie, has a good neighbor, Bonita. They often trade dishes and recipes. This is the latest one that Jodie sent to me.

Blend cake mix, butter, coconut and egg with an electric mixer on low speed until mixture is crumbly. Lightly press mixture into an ungreased 9x13 inch baking pan, or use a springform pan and make it like a cheesecake.

To make filling, beat together cream cheese, eggs, sugar and vanilla until smooth and fluffy. Spread filling over crust. Bake at 350 degrees for 20 to 25 minutes.

While baking, prepare topping. Mix sour cream, sugar and vanilla until smooth. Spread topping over cheesecake immediately after removing from oven. Cool. Refrigerate at least 8 hours before serving.

This cake is nothing unusual. However, the icing is the best and would make a simple cake turn into a very special one!

Praline Cake

Cake

1	18 ounce box butter recipe cake mix
1	teaspoon vanilla butter and nut flavoring

Icing

1¼	cups water
3	cups sugar
1	stick margarine or butter
1	cup evaporated milk
3	cups ground pecans
1	teaspoon vanilla butter and nut flavoring

Prepare cake mix according to package directions, adding flavoring to batter. Bake in 2 layer cake pans. Cool. Split layers in half horizontally, resulting in 4 layers.

For icing, cook water and sugar in a saucepan until a drop forms a hard ball in a cup of cold water. Add margarine and milk and cook to soft ball stage. Remove from heat and add pecans and flavoring. Stir until mixture reaches a spreading consistency. (If icing becomes too thick, add a little hot water.) Spread icing between layers and on top and sides of cake.

Banana Nut Loaf (in a jar)

1	stick butter or margarine, softened
2	cups sugar
2	eggs, room temperature
2	cups mashed bananas (about 6 bananas)
3	cups all-purpose flour
½	teaspoon salt
1½	teaspoon baking soda
½	cup buttermilk
½-1	cup chopped nuts
1	teaspoon vanilla

Cream together butter and sugar. Add eggs and beat until smooth. Mix in bananas. Combine flour and salt. Dissolve baking soda in buttermilk. Add dry ingredients and buttermilk mixture, alternately, to creamed mixture. Stir in nuts and vanilla. Pour batter into 6 wide-mouth jars that have been sprayed with PAM, filling jars to 1-cup level. Bake at 350 degrees for 40 to 50 minutes or until a knife inserted in the center comes out clean. Seal jars immediately after removing from oven and turn jars upside down. Enjoy!

If you don't have buttermilk, substitute sour milk. For sour milk, measure 1 tablespoon vinegar into a measuring cup. Add milk to equal ½ cup. Let stand a few minutes.

If this isn't the ultimate! What a unique way to bake a cake. This works great for gifts at Christmas for those special people you wish to remember. Simply tie a ribbon around the jar and watch the surprised looks on your friends' faces! Thank you, Miss Doris, for sharing with me and being my friend.

Strawberry Pecan Cake

Batter

1	18 ounce box white cake mix
1	3 ounce box strawberry gelatin
¾	cup vegetable oil
4	eggs
½	cup milk
1	cup chopped pecans
1	cup frozen strawberries, thawed
1	cup coconut

Filling

1	16 ounce package powdered sugar
1	stick margarine
½	cup chopped pecans
½	cup coconut
½	cup frozen strawberries, thawed and drained, juice reserved

Combine cake mix and gelatin. Add oil. Add eggs, one at a time, beating well after each addition. Mix in milk, pecans, strawberries and coconut. Pour batter into greased and floured cake pans. Bake at 350 degrees until done.

For filling, cream powdered sugar and margarine. Add pecans, coconut and strawberries. Add reserved strawberry juice as needed to reach a spreading consistency. Spread filling between layers and on top of cake when cooled.

Lemon Torte

Meringue Shell

6	egg whites
¾	teaspoon cream of tartar
1	teaspoon vanilla
1½	cups sugar
2	tablespoons sliced almonds

Lemon Custard

6	egg yolks
½	cup sugar
¼	cup lemon juice
2	tablespoons lemon zest
10	drops yellow food coloring
1	12 ounce container Cool Whip, thawed

Beat egg whites with cream of tartar and vanilla until soft peaks form. Gradually beat in sugar until glossy with stiff peaks. Spread mixture in three 9 inch cake pans with removable bottoms. Sprinkle one pan of meringue with almonds. Bake at 300 degrees for 45 minutes. Turn off oven and leave meringue in oven for 3 hours or overnight. Remove from pans.

To make custard, beat egg yolks until lemon colored. Add sugar, lemon juice and zest and food coloring. Cook in a double boiler over low heat, stirring occasionally, until thick. Cool thoroughly. Fold cooled custard into Cool Whip. Spread half of custard over one of the plain meringue shells. Place second plain shell on top. Spread remaining custard over second plain shell. Top with meringue shell with almonds. Refrigerate until serving time. Serves 12.

Cannoli

Filling

3	pounds ricotta cheese
2½	cups powdered sugar
¼	cup semisweet chocolate chips or grated sweet chocolate
2	tablespoons chopped citron
10	candied cherries, finely chopped
½	teaspoon cinnamon

Cannoli Shells

3	cups sifted all-purpose flour
1	tablespoon sugar
¼	teaspoon cinnamon
¾	cup port
	vegetable oil or shortening for deep frying
1	egg yolk, slightly beaten

Garnish

chopped pistachio nuts
powdered sugar

In a large bowl, beat ricotta cheese with an electric mixer for 1 minute. Add powdered sugar and beat 1 minute or until light and creamy. Add chocolate, citron, cherries and cinnamon. Beat on low speed until well blended. Cover and refrigerate at least 2 hours or until well chilled.

While filling chills, prepare cannoli shells. Sift together flour, sugar and cinnamon onto a board. Make a well in the center and fill with port. With a fork, gradually blend flour into port. When dough is stiff enough to handle, knead 15 minutes or until dough is smooth and stiff. If dough is too moist and sticky, knead in a little more sifted flour. Cover and refrigerate dough for 2 hours.

When ready to cook, slowly heat 3 to 4 inches of oil in a deep-fat fryer, electric skillet or heavy saucepan to 400 degrees. Meanwhile, on a lightly floured surface, roll one-third of dough to paper thinness, making a 16 inch round. Cut into eight 5 inch circles. Wrap a circle loosely around a 6 inch long, 1 inch diameter cannoli form or dowel. Seal

(continued on next page)

Cannoli *(continued)*

with beaten egg yolk. Gently drop dough-covered forms, two at a time, into hot oil. Fry 1 minute or until browned on all sides, turning if necessary. Remove with a tongs and drain on paper towels. Carefully remove forms. Repeat until all dough is used. Shells can be made a day or two ahead and stored, covered, at room temperature.

Just before serving, with a teaspoon or small spatula, fill shells with filling. Garnish ends with chopped pistachio nuts and sprinkle powdered sugar on top. Makes 24.

Spumoni

3	**pints chocolate ice cream, slightly softened**
1	**pint pistachio ice cream, slightly softened**
2	**pints vanilla ice cream, slightly softened**
1	**cup candied mixed fruit**
2	**teaspoons rum flavoring**
1½	**cups heavy whipping cream, whipped**

Place a 2½ quart melon mold in the freezer. In a large bowl, beat chocolate ice cream with an electric mixer until smooth but not melted. With a spoon, quickly press ice cream evenly inside the chilled melon mold. Freeze until firm.

In a medium bowl, beat pistachio ice cream until smooth. Press evenly over chocolate layer. Freeze until firm.

In a large bowl, combine vanilla ice cream, candied fruit and rum flavoring. Beat well until blended but not melted. Press mixture into center of mold. Freeze until firm.

To unmold, let spumoni stand at room temperature for 5 minutes. Invert onto a serving plate. Hold a hot, damp dishcloth over mold and shake to release. Return to freezer until the surface is firm. Spread three-fourths of whipped cream over mold. Pipe remaining whipped cream through a pastry bag with a decorating tip onto spumoni. Return to freezer until serving time. Serves 16 to 20.

A viewer asked me if I had a cracker pudding recipe. Well, not only did I not have one, I did not know what she was talking about — Cajuns in Gueydan apparently never made cracker puddings. So she sent me this recipe.

Old-Fashioned Cracker Pudding

Custard

25	unsalted crackers
2	cups boiling water
1	cup sugar
1	stick butter or margarine, softened
4	eggs yolks
1	cup whole milk
1	cup evaporated milk
2	teaspoons vanilla

Meringue

4	egg whites
1	cup sugar
2	teaspoons almond extract

Soak crackers in boiling water in a greased baking dish. In a mixing bowl, cream sugar, butter and egg yolks with an electric mixer until light and lemon colored. Scald whole and evaporated milk; do not boil. Add egg mixture to hot milk, stirring constantly. Add vanilla and pour hot custard over soaking crackers. Stir well. Place baking dish in a larger pan of water. Bake at 350 degrees for 30 to 40 minutes.

To make meringue, beat egg whites until very stiff. Beat in sugar. Add almond extract and beat to mix. Pour meringue over the baked pudding. Return to oven and bake until meringue is brown. Cool. Refrigerate.

Lemon Sauce

¼-½	cup sugar
1	tablespoon cornstarch
1	cup water
2-3	tablespoons butter
½	teaspoon lemon zest
1½	tablespoons lemon juice

Combine sugar and cornstarch in a saucepan. Stir in water and bring to a boil. Cook, stirring constantly, until thickened. Stir in butter and lemon zest and juice.

Rum Sauce

⅓   cup sugar
⅓   cup cornstarch
2   cups evaporated milk
1   teaspoon vanilla
2   tablespoons butter, melted
⅓   cup rum

Mix sugar and cornstarch in a saucepan. Add milk, vanilla and butter. Bring to a boil and cook, stirring constantly, until sauce thickens. Remove from heat and add rum. Serve over pudding or plain cake. Makes 4 cups.

These sauces are delicious served on bread puddings or cakes.

Lemon Custard

4   eggs
      few grains of salt
1¾   cups sugar
4   tablespoons butter
2   tablespoons lemon zest
½   cup lemon juice

Beat eggs well in the top of a double boiler. Add salt. Blend in sugar and beat until creamy. Add butter and heat in double boiler until thickened. Remove from heat and stir in lemon zest and juice. Whip well until blended.

I went to Kent House in Alexandria to cook catfish courtbouillion on an open hearth. I had never done that before, but I really enjoyed it. Besides, the ladies there are so very nice. They fixed this for dessert — so soft, smooth and light — and so delicious!

Tips for Fluffy Meringue

1 Use large fresh eggs. Allow the egg whites to reach room temperature before beating them.

2 Spread meringue over pie filling to edges of crust. Then meringue won't pull away from the crust as it bakes.

3 Always allow the pie filling to cool before topping with meringue.

4 Bake meringue at 400 degrees on center rack for 8 to 10 minutes.

5 Meringue should be cooled slowly. A draft causes meringues to shrivel and form little beads of syrup on top.

6 Meringue will not stick to a knife if the knife is dipped into water before cutting pie pieces.

7 To keep meringue from weeping, follow these "3 nevers":

Never add more than 2 tablespoons sugar for each egg white.

Never bake above 425 degrees.

Never cool quickly.

Tips for Baking Perfect Pastry

1 Use ovenproof glass pans for a well baked, browned undercrust. Shiny metal doesn't bake the undercrust as well because it reflects heat. Aluminum pans with satiny finish also give good results.

2 Pierce crust all over with a fork to permit air to escape and to prevent blisters.

3 Cool thoroughly before pouring in filling.

4 Bake on shelf above center at 425 degrees for 12 minutes or until golden brown.

5 To keep crust from "soaking":

For fruit pies, spread a little dry sugar and flour over bottom crust before adding fruit.

For custard pies, brush unbaked crust with a little beaten egg and let dry in refrigerator for 10 minutes before adding filling for baking.

Tips for 2 Crust Pies

1 Cut at least 4 slits in top crust to let steam escape or top crust will puff up leaving a hollow space underneath.

2 Fold edge of upper pastry under lower edge before fluting to keep juices from boiling out.

3 Bake at 450 degrees for first 10 to 15 minutes, then reduce temperature to 325 degrees for remainder of cooking time.

Pecan Pie

⅔	**cup sugar**
½	**teaspoon salt**
1	**tablespoons cornstarch**
3	**eggs, beaten**
1	**tablespoon vanilla**
5	**tablespoons butter, melted**
1	**cup corn syrup**
1	**cup broken pecans**
1	**pie shell, unbaked**

Mix sugar, salt and cornstarch. Add eggs, vanilla, butter and corn syrup. Beat mixture together well. Stir in pecans. Pour mixture into an unbaked pie shell. Place in a preheated 375 degree oven. Immediately reduce oven temperature to 350 degrees. Bake about 45 minutes. Serves 6.

My brother told me that he had tasted a pecan pie that was even better than mine! So I simply had to get this recipe! My cousin, Jay, married a lovely lady who is a great cook. They were 72 years young and celebrated their first anniversary in January. He and Bernice have never been happier. It is true that the way to a man's heart is through his stomach!

This is a very unusual recipe which I acquired in high school. I have not enjoyed it for a long time, but really plan on introducing it to my granddaughter so she can bake it for me.

Raisin Pie

1	cup sugar
2	eggs, beaten
1	stick margarine, melted
1	teaspoon vanilla
⅔	cup chopped pecans
⅔	cup coconut
⅔	cup raisins
2	tablespoons vinegar
	pinch of salt
1	pie shell, unbaked

Mix sugar and eggs. Add margarine and vanilla and mix thoroughly. Add pecans, coconut, raisins, vinegar and salt. Mix well and pour into unbaked pie shell. Bake at 350 degrees for 35 to 40 minutes.

A friend of mine from Monroe, Amanda Dean, sent me this recipe. Her aunt, the late Jane Burnsicle Earnest, had given it to her. It is very unusual but tasty as well.

Cracker Pie

3	egg whites
1	teaspoon cream of tartar
1	cup sugar
1	teaspoon vanilla
1	cup pecans
16	soda crackers, coarsely crushed
1	pint heavy whipping cream
½	cup coconut

Beat egg whites with cream of tartar until stiff and dry. Fold in sugar, vanilla, pecans and cracker crumbs. Pour into an 8x8 inch pan which has been sprayed with PAM. Bake at 375 degrees for 20 minutes or until dry and crusty. Cool. Whip cream and spread over pie. Sprinkle coconut on top.

Nutter Butter Peanut Butter Pie

Crust

24	Nutter Butter sandwich cookies
5	tablespoons butter, melted

Filling

1	8 ounce package cream cheese, softened
1	cup creamy peanut butter
¾	cup sugar
1	tablespoon vanilla
1	8 ounce container Cool Whip, thawed, divided

Crush cookies in a zip-top plastic bag with a rolling pin or in a food processor. Mix cookie crumbs and butter. Press mixture into the bottom and up the sides of a 9 inch pie plate.

To make filling, mix cream cheese, peanut butter, sugar and vanilla with an electric mixer on medium speed until well blended. Gently stir in 1½ cups Cool Whip. Spoon mixture over crust. Freeze 4 hours or overnight until firm. To serve, let pie stand at room temperature for 30 minutes or until it can be easily cut. Garnish with remaining Cool Whip and additional cookies, if desired.

Special extra: Just before serving, drizzle chocolate-flavored syrup on plates.

I went to Houma to film on location. While there, I visited with some of my friends. I brought crawfish for an étouffée which I cooked (with Missy's help) for my friends, Arthur and Shirley. While I was there, one of Shirley's friends, Lemora, came in with this delicious peanut butter pie — it was the best I ever tasted and I give a lot of credit to the crust.

Surprise Pie

3	egg whites
½	teaspoon cream of tartar
1	cup sugar
1	teaspoon vanilla
36	Ritz crackers, very finely crushed
1	cup chopped pecans

Beat egg whites until foamy. Add cream of tartar and beat until very stiff. Add sugar and vanilla. Fold in cracker crumbs. Fold in pecans last. Pour into a pie plate. Bake at 350 degrees for 30 minutes.

I always wondered what recipe Piccadilly Cafeterias used to make a very delicious pie which I always put on my tray. Little did I know that I had that exact recipe in my old recipe file from my high school days.

This is a family favorite which has been a tradition for years. I had rather use the fresh pumpkin but for holidays, I sometimes use the canned due to lack of time. Regardless, it is really good!

Pumpkin Pie

1	1¾ pound fresh sugar baby pumpkin, or 1 (30 ounce) can
⅔	cup sugar
1	teaspoon cinnamon
¼	teaspoon ginger
¼	teaspoon freshly ground nutmeg
1½	cup evaporated milk
3	eggs, lightly beaten
1	pie shell, unbaked
	Cool Whip for topping

Cut fresh pumpkin into large pieces, discarding seeds and pith. Steam pumpkin in a double boiler or spaghetti cooker for 30 minutes or until pulp is soft. Cool and scrape pulp from the skin. Purée pulp in a food processor or blender until smooth. Stir in sugar, cinnamon, ginger, nutmeg, milk and eggs. Mix well. Pour mixture into unbaked pie shell. Bake at 350 degrees for 40 to 45 minutes or until filling is set. Top with Cool Whip.

This is an all American favorite. It's easy and delicious. Don't forget the Cool Whip (a dab will do it.) Or even better, a scoop of the ice cream on next page.

Sweet Potato Pie

2	cups cooked and mashed sweet potatoes
5	tablespoons margarine, melted
3	egg, beaten
⅓	cup milk or half-and-half
½	teaspoon baking powder
1	cup sugar
	pinch of salt
1	teaspoon allspice
1	teaspoon cinnamon
1	pie shell, unbaked

Combine all ingredients except pie shell in a bowl. Beat well with an electric mixer. Pour mixture into an unbaked pie shell. Bake at 350 degrees for about 50 to 60 minutes.

Sweet Potato Ice Cream

4	eggs, separated
2	cups sugar
1	12 ounce can evaporated milk
1	14 ounce can sweetened condensed milk
1	tablespoon vanilla
3	cups cooked, drained and creamed sweet potatoes
8	cups milk

Beat egg whites until stiff. Add yolks and remaining ingredients, beating after each addition. Freeze in a hand or electric ice cream freezer. Makes 6 quarts.

The first time I ate this, I could not believe it and how good it was. Who would even think of putting sweet potatoes in ice cream? It works!

Cherry Pie

1	cup sugar
¼	cup flour
½	cup water
3	cups Bing cherries
1	teaspoon almond flavoring
1	double pie crust, unbaked
1	teaspoon butter
1	tablespoon water
1	tablespoon sugar

Mix 1 cup sugar and flour in a saucepan. Add ½ cup water and stir until sugar dissolves. Bring to a boil. Add cherries and cook until a syrup forms. Remove from heat and add almond flavoring. Pour filling into the bottom pie crust. Dot with butter. Lay top crust over filling and seal all around the edges. Cut slits in top crust. Bake at 350 degrees for 45 minutes. Mix 1 tablespoon water and 1 tablespoon sugar. Baste crust with sugar water and bake 15 minutes longer. Cool.

Cherry pie is my son's favorite. He really enjoys it plain, but prefers to top his slice of pie with a huge scoop of vanilla ice cream. Umm! Even though he is grown and away from home, I try to have one for him when he comes for a visit.

To "cobble up" means to put together in a hurry. And that's exactly how I do my cobblers. These are always good but even better with vanilla ice cream!

Blackberry Cobbler

Pastry

1	cup flour
½	teaspoon salt
⅓	cup shortening or butter
2	tablespoons cold water

Filling

¾	cup sugar
1	tablespoon cornstarch
⅛	teaspoon salt
5	cups fresh blackberries, washed and drained
2	tablespoons margarine or butter
1	tablespoon water
1	tablespoon sugar

Mix flour and salt in a bowl. Cut in shortening with a pastry blender or 2 table knives. Sprinkle with cold water and stir with a fork. Roll out dough on a lightly floured surface. Transfer pastry to a 9 inch square baking dish and trim edges, reserving leftover dough. Set aside.

To prepare filling, combine ¾ cup sugar, cornstarch and salt. Sprinkle mixture over berries and gently mix well. Pour berries over pastry in baking dish. Dot with margarine. Roll out leftover dough and cut into strips. Lay pastry strips across berries. Brush strips with a mixture of 1 tablespoon water and 1 tablespoon sugar. Bake at 425 degrees for 30 minutes. Serves 6.

For a peach cobbler, simply use 2 cups peaches instead of the blackberries.

Pineapple Chiffon Pie

1	8 ounce can crushed pineapple, liquid reserved
1	envelope unflavored gelatin
3	eggs, separated
¼	cup sugar
1	tablespoon lemon zest
3	tablespoons lemon juice
¼	teaspoon salt
½	cup sugar
1	9 inch pie shell, baked
1	cup whipped cream
	chopped nuts for decoration (optional)

Drain pineapple, reserving liquid. Add enough cold water to reserved liquid to equal ¼ cup. Soften gelatin in liquid mixture. Beat egg yolks. Add ¼ cup sugar. Mix in pineapple, lemon zest and lemon juice. Cook mixture in the top of a double boiler over hot water, stirring until thickened. Add softened gelatin and stir until dissolved. Cool in refrigerator until mixture starts to thicken. Beat egg whites until stiff. Fold whites into pineapple mixture along with salt and ½ cup sugar. Pour mixture into baked pie shell. Chill 3 hours. Top with whipped cream and nuts.

I enjoy most any kind of pie but this is my favorite! I have been making these since high school and use the original recipe - can't improve on perfection. It is so light and delightful!

Peach Cobbler

2	double crust pie shells, unbaked, divided
⅔	cup sugar
2	tablespoons flour
¼	teaspoon freshly ground nutmeg
3	cups sliced peaches

Use a whole double crust to line the bottom of a 9x13 inch baking pan or dish. Mix sugar, flour and nutmeg. Pour mixture over peaches and mix until peaches are coated. Pour peaches over crust in pan. Cut remaining whole double crust into ¼ inch wide strips. Lay pastry strips along and across the top of peach filling. Bake at 375 degrees for 1 hour. Top with ice cream or Cool Whip.

This can be served as a cobbler or as a deep-dish pie. I love to bake these not only because they taste so good but they are so easy to make. I use canned peaches when I don't have the fresh ones but remember to drain them. This dessert has always been a big hit at family outings or church functions.

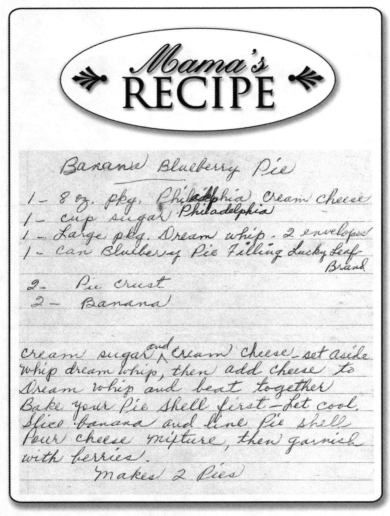

Mama's RECIPE

Banana Blueberry Pie

1 – 8 oz. pkg. Philadelphia Cream cheese
1 – cup sugar
1 – Large pkg. Dream whip – 2 envelopes
1 – can Blueberry Pie Filling Lucky Leaf Brand

2 – Pie crust
2 – Banana

cream sugar and cream cheese – set aside
whip dream whip, then add cheese to
Dream whip and beat together
Bake your Pie shell first – Let cool.
Slice banana and line Pie shell
Pour cheese mixture, then garnish
with berries.
makes 2 Pies

Banana Blueberry Pie —This one out of Mama's file box
is very unique — and delicious!

Pie

1 can condensed milk
1 " pink lemonade
1 tool-whip 4½ oz.

Mama's Lemon Pie — This was so simple that Mama did not need directions. Just mix and throw (pour) into baked pie crust. It was her favorite!

A year ago I had the pleasure of staying at Bobby De Bleux Bed and Breakfast in Natchitoches. I was doing my Christmas special in the City of Lights. Bobby served his guests and me this wonderful treat — it was the first time I had ever eaten a poached pear. This year for Christmas, I served it to my family.

Poached Pears

4	pears
1	tablespoon lemon juice
1½	cups white Zinfandel wine
1½	cups sugar
2	teaspoons vanilla
4	sprigs fresh mint

Peel pears, leaving stems intact. Remove cores from bottom of pears. In a saucepan, combine lemon juice, wine, sugar and vanilla. Bring to a boil and simmer 5 minutes, stirring frequently. Add pears to saucepan, stem-side up. Simmer, basting frequently, for 15 to 20 minutes or until the wine mixture thickens to a syrup consistency and the pears are tender. Transfer pears to individual serving bowls. Cook syrup, stirring frequently, until reduced. Pour syrup over each pear. Slice into bite-size pieces and decorate with mint sprigs. Enjoy!

Boston Cream Pie

Cake

3	eggs, separated
1	teaspoon vanilla
½	cup sugar
	pinch of salt
¾	cup cake flour

Filling

½	cup sugar
¼	cup all-purpose flour
1½	cups milk
6	egg yolks
2	teaspoons vanilla
	pinch of salt

(continued on next page)

Boston Cream Pie *(continued)*

Glaze

½   cup sugar

3   tablespoons light corn syrup

2   tablespoons water

4   ounces (4 squares) semisweet chocolate, coarsely chopped

To make cake, beat together egg yolks and vanilla with an electric mixer on medium speed until blended. Beat in half of sugar until very thick and pale. Using clean, dry beaters, beat together egg whites and salt at medium speed until very soft peaks form. Gradually beat in remaining sugar until stiff, but not dry, peaks form. Fold yolk mixture into egg whites. Sift cake flour over mixture and fold gently to mix; do not overmix. Pour batter into a greased and wax paper-lined 9 inch round cake pan. Bake at 350 degrees for 25 minutes or until top springs back when lightly pressed. Loosen cake by running a metal spatula around sides of pan. Invert cake onto a wire rack. Remove pan, leaving wax paper on cake. Turn cake right side up. Cool completely on rack.

Meanwhile, prepare filling. In a saucepan, mix together sugar and flour. Gradually whisk in milk, then egg yolks, vanilla and salt. Bring to a boil over medium heat. Boil for 1 minute, whisking constantly. Strain through a fine sieve into a bowl. Press plastic wrap onto surface and chill 30 minutes.

Using a serrated knife, cut cake horizontally in half, forming two circles. Carefully remove wax paper. Place one cake circle on a serving plate. Spread filling evenly over cake. Top with remaining cake circle.

To prepare glaze, in a saucepan, bring sugar, corn syrup and water to a boil over low heat, stirring constantly, until sugar dissolves. Remove from heat. Add chocolate and let stand 1 minute. Stir until smooth. Slowly pour glaze over top of cake, allowing it to drip down sides. Let stand until glaze sets. Serves 8.

I really enjoy Boston Cream Pies. They make perfect desserts after a hearty meal! My 3 children always enjoyed my baking these. And they still do! I have used this recipe for years. Is this a pie or a cake?

Champagne Punch

Frozen Ring

1	cup pineapple juice
1	cup orange juice
1	cup water
1	banana, sliced
1	cup strawberries, sliced

Combine frozen ring ingredients and pour into a ring or mold. Freeze until ready to use.

Punch

2½	cups frozen strawberries, thawed
6½	cups rose wine, chilled
¾	cup frozen lemonade concentrate, thawed
3¼	cups champagne, chilled

Mix together all punch ingredients. Pour over frozen ring in a punch bowl and serve immediately.

Brandy Ice

6	ounces brandy
2	ounces crème de cacao
4	large scoops vanilla ice cream

Combine all ingredients in a blender and mix until blended. Serve in champagne glasses. Makes 6 to 8.

Green Punch
1 qt. Lime Sherbet
2 - 6 oz. can frozen Lemon Juice Concentrate
2 - 6 oz. frozen Lime Juice Concentrate
6 - juice cans of water
4 qts. Gingerale chilled
Food Coloring, green

This was my Mama's favorite punch. She always enjoyed fixing it as well as drinking it at parties. I have had this recipe ever since she made it for my sixteenth birthday party — that was a long time ago!

Cooking Terms

Bake —To cook by dry heat, usually in an oven.

Baste — To moisten foods during cooking with pan drippings or a special sauce to add flavor and to prevent drying.

Beat — To make a mixture smooth by adding air with a brisk whipping or stirring motion, using a spoon or an electric mixer.

Blanch —To precook in boiling water or steam to prepare foods for canning or freezing, or to loosen their skins.

Blend — To process food in an electric blender. Or, to thoroughly combine two or more ingredients by hand with a stirring motion to make a smooth and uniform mixture.

Boil —To cook in liquid at boiling temperature where bubbles rise to the surface and break. For a full, rolling boil, bubbles form rapidly throughout the mixture.

Braise — To cook slowly with a small amount of liquid in a tightly covered pan on top of the range or in the oven.

Bread — To coat with bread crumbs before cooking.

Broil — To cook by direct heat, usually in a broiler or over coals.

Butterfly — To split foods such as shrimp and steak through the middle without completely separating sections and then spreading the sections to resemble a butterfly.

Caramelize — To melt sugar slowly over low heat until it becomes brown in color.

Chop — To cut into pieces about the size of peas with a knife, chopper, blender or food processor.

Coat — To evenly cover food with crumbs, flour or a batter.

Cream — To beat a mixture with a spoon or electric mixer till it becomes soft and smooth. When applied to combining shortening and sugar, the mixture is beaten till light and fluffy, depending on the proportion of sugar to shortening.

Crisp-tender —To cook food to the stage where it is tender but still crisp.

Cube — To cut into pieces that are the same size on each side — at least half an inch.

Cut in — To mix shortening with dry ingredients using a pastry blender or two knives.

Dab — A small amount; more than a dash.

Dash — ⅛ teaspoon of dry ingredients or liquids.

Dice — To cut food into small cubes of uniform size and shape — between ⅛ and ¼ inch.

Dredge — To coat with flour or sugar.

Dust —To sprinkle foods lightly with sugar, flour, etc.

Fillet — To cut lean meat or fish into pieces without bones.

Finely shred — To rub food across a fine shredding surface to form very narrow strips.

Fold — To add ingredients gently to a mixture. Using a spatula, cut down through the mixture; cut across the bottom of the bowl, and then up and over, close to the surface. Turn the bowl frequently for even distribution.

Fry — To cook in hot fat. To panfry, cook food in a small amount of fat. To deep-fat fry, cook the food immersed in a large amount of fat.

Grate — To rub food across a grating surface that separates the food into very fine particles.

Grill — To cook food over hot coals.

Grind — To use a food grinder to cut a food into very fine pieces.

Julienne — To cut vegetables, fruits or meats into matchlike strips.

Knead — To work dough with the heel of your hand in a pressing and folding motion.

Marinate — To allow a food to stand in a liquid to add flavor.

Mince — To chop food into very small, irregularly shaped pieces.

Mix — To stir together evenly.

Panbroil — To cook uncovered, removing fat as it accumulates.

Panfry — To cook food in a small amount of hot fat.

Peel — To remove the outer layer or skin from a fruit or vegetable.

Poach — To cook food in hot liquid, being careful that the food holds its shape while cooking.

Sauté — To brown or cook food in a small amount of hot fat.

Scald — To bring food to a temperature just below boiling so that tiny bubbles form at the edges of the pan.

Sear — To brown the surface of meat by quick application of intense heat, usually in a hot pot, pan or hot oven.

Shred — To rub food on a shredder to form long, narrow pieces.

Sift — To put one one or more dry ingredients through a sieve or sifter to incorporate air and break up lumps.

Simmer — To cook food in liquid over low heat at a temperature of 185-210 degrees F. (85-99 degrees C.) where bubbles form at a slow rate and burst before reaching the surface.

Sliver — To cut or shred into lengths.

Steam — To cook food in steam. A small amount of boiling water is used and more water is added during steaming if necessary.

Stew — To simmer cooked food slowly in a small amount of liquid.

Stir — To mix ingredients with a spoon in a circular or figure-eight motion till well combined.

Stir-fry — To cook food quickly in a small amount of hot fat, stirring constantly.

Toss — To mix ingredients lightly by lifting and dropping them with a spoon or a spoon and fork.

Whip — To beat food lightly and rapidly, incorporating air into the mixture to make it light and to increase volume.

Glossary

ANDOUILLE: A popular reddish Cajun pork sausage made from pork stomach and other ingredients.

APPETIZER: A snack.

BISQUE: A popular Cajun soup often made with crawfish, in which the crawfish heads are stuffed with meat of the tails and placed in the soup bowl.

BOUCHERIE: A great Cajun tradition whereby groups of families got together once a week to butcher one or more calves or pigs, thereafter dividing the various cuts and making various Cajun dishes such as boudin, hogshead cheese and cracklins from portions of the pigs.

BOUDIN: A popular Cajun pork sausage, usually light in color, made with various parts of pork and rice.

BRUNCH: Some meal that Cajuns do not have.

CAJUN MUSIC: Strictly Cajun French with one-step, two-step and jitterbug dancing. Bands consists of an accordian player, a guitar player, a violin player and a drummer. Sometimes a steel guitar player or vocalist who also plays an instrument, is added. (Cajun bands are mostly made up of family members.)

CORNICHON: Cucumber strips soaked in vinegar with hot peppers.

COURTBOUILLION: A light Cajun fish soup including tomatoes and served with rice.

CRACKLINS: A dish made by frying small cut portions of pork skin and pork fat; also called "gratons."

CRAWFISH: A plentiful Louisiana crustacean used in many classic Cajun dishes, which looks like a small lobster.

ETOUFFEE: A method of Cajun food preparation meaning smothered and cooked without a roux; used to cook crawfish, fish and other dishes.

EXACT MEASUREMENTS: Just enough — not too much!

FILÉ: A ground sassafras leaf. Used to season and thicken gumbo. (Always add to gumbo just before it is served, preferably in a plate or bowl of gumbo.)

FRICASSEE: A Cajun stew made with a roux and chicken, duck, venison, beef or other meats and served over rice.

GREEN ONIONS: A very commonly used seasoning in Cajun dishes; also sometimes referred to as green onion tops by the Cajuns.

GUMBO: A soup or stew usually made with a roux and including meats commonly available in Cajun country, such as fowl, game, Cajun sausage, tasso, or seafoods.

JAMBALAYA: A Cajun dish in which pork, game and various other ingredients are cooked together with rice.

LAGNIAPPE: A French word meaning something extra or in addition to or including other things.

OKRA: A green pod vegetable of African origin used in gumbos and as a side dish.

PIROGUE: A small, narrow wooden boat resembling a canoe in structure, used in the bayou.

ROUX: A classic Cajun concoction made by blending flour and oil and cooking the two together; used in Cajun gumbos, stews fricassees, courtbouillons, sauce piquantes and other dishes.

SALT MEAT: A salty pork meat often used to season Cajun soups and other dishes.

SAUCE: A gravy.

SAUCE PIQUANT: A hot, spicy Cajun stew made with a roux, tomato sauce and various meats such as hen, geese, duck, rabbits, squirrel or turtle and other meats historically available in Cajun country.

SAUSAGE CASING: A natural casing used in the preparation of boudin, andouille and pork sausages made from the intestines of pork and beef and readily available at most meat markets.

TASSO: A dried, smoked pork used in gumbos and other dishes.

ZYDECO MUSIC: A blend of Cajun, jazz, rock, soul and country music creating a whole new style of dancing to a different beat.

This for That

Instead of this:	Use this:
1 teaspoon onion powder	2 teaspoons baking powder
1 clove fresh garlic	⅛ teaspoon garlic powder
1 tablespoon fresh herbs	1 teaspoon ground or crush herbs
1 teaspoon lemon juice	½ teaspoon vinegar

MILK

1 cup fresh, whole	1 cup laso fat plus 2 tablespoons butter
1 cup whole	½ cup evaporated milk plus ½ cup water
1 cup skim	4 tablespoons nonfat dry milk plus 1 cup water

CREAM

1 cup coffee cream	3 tablespoons butter plus 7/8 cup milk
1 cup heavy cream	⅓ cup butter plus ¾ cup milk
1 cup half and half	1½ tablespoon butter plus 7/8 cup milk
1 cup sour to equal one cup	1 tablespoon lemon juice plus plus evaporated milk
1 cup whipping	⅓ cup butter plus ¾ cup milk

HONEY

1 cup	1-1¼ cups sugar plus ¼ cup liquid

YEAST

1 cake compressed	1 package or 2 teaspoons active dry yeast

SUGAR

1 tablespoon maple	1 teaspoon white granulated sugar
1 cup maple	1 cup brown sugar
1 cup bread crumbs	¾ cup cracker crumbs

MUSHROOMS

1 pound fresh	6 ounces canned mushrooms

TOMATOES

1 cup, packed	½ cup tomato sauce plus ½ cup water
1 cup, juice	½ cup tomato sauce plus ½ cup water
2 cups, sauce	¾ cup tomato paste plus 1 cup water

BUTTER

1 cup butter	1 cup margarine
	⅞ cup clarified bacon fat or drippings (for sautéing)
	⅞ cup lard or solid shortening

CHOCOLATE

1 square	¼ cup cocoa
1 ounce square, unsweetened	3 tablespoons cocoa plus 1 tablespoon shortening

FLOUR

1 cup all purpose	1 cup plus 2 tablespoons cake flour
1 cup cake flour	⅞ cup all purpose flour
1 cup self-rising	1 cup all purpose plus 1 teaspoon baking powder and ½ teaspoon salt
1 tablespoon for thickening or 1 tablespoon tapioca	½ tablespoon corn starch, potato starch or rice starch
1 tablespoon corn starch	2 tablespoons flour (for thickening)

Notes

A

Classic CAJUN
P.O. Box 3 • Jones, LA 71250

Please send _____ copies of *Classic Cajun* @ $16.95 each _____
_____ copies of *Classic Cajun Deux* @ $16.95 each _____
Postage and handling @ $ 3.50 each _____
Louisiana residents add sales tax @ $ 1.19 each _____
TOTAL _____

Name _____

Address _____

City _____ State _____ Zip _____

Make checks payable to Classic Cajun or call 800/257-5829 (LUCY)
www.mslucy.com

Classic CAJUN
P.O. Box 3 • Jones, LA 71250

Please send _____ copies of *Classic Cajun* @ $16.95 each _____
_____ copies of *Classic Cajun Deux* @ $16.95 each _____
Postage and handling @ $ 3.50 each _____
Louisiana residents add sales tax @ $ 1.19 each _____
TOTAL _____

Name _____

Address _____

City _____ State _____ Zip _____

Make checks payable to Classic Cajun or call 800/257-5829 (LUCY)
www.mslucy.com

Classic CAJUN
P.O. Box 3 • Jones, LA 71250

Please send _____ copies of *Classic Cajun* @ $16.95 each _____
_____ copies of *Classic Cajun Deux* @ $16.95 each _____
Postage and handling @ $ 3.50 each _____
Louisiana residents add sales tax @ $ 1.19 each _____
TOTAL _____

Name _____

Address _____

City _____ State _____ Zip _____

Make checks payable to Classic Cajun or call 800/257-5829 (LUCY)
www.mslucy.com